Moffat Miscellany
Volume 1

Early Visitors and Their Impressions of Moffat

Jim Storrar

April 2008

Contents

To Sandie, Tom, Ellen, Biz, and dear friends in Moffat.

Thank you for your patience, help and encouragement.

Preface

"The present is the key to the past and the past is the key to the future."
(*James Hutton*)

This is the first volume in a series entitled "Moffat Miscellany". The series is dedicated to the people of Moffat, to all those who know it and love it, and to those who know it but perhaps have less regard for it. It is also dedicated to others who have written about Moffat and upon whose knowledge and inspiration I have drawn so freely. In particular, I am indebted to Emilio "Jock" Dicerbo, Drew Grieve, Jane Boyd, W.A.J. Prevost, Sheila Forman, John T. Johnstone, Agnes Marchbank, John Brown, Charles Stewart, William Keddie, and John McDiarmid. My thanks also go to the staff of the Ewart Library in Dumfries, Moffat Library, the National Archives of Scotland, and the British Library, for their unfailing patience, courtesy, and expertise.

Moffat's history is extraordinarily rich and I hope that Moffat Miscellany will stimulate further interest in that history. I had intended to limit the series to the geographical area of the Parish of Moffat but, although Moffat lies at the heart of things, I have been unable to resist making occasional forays into the nearby Parishes of Wamphray, Kirkpatrick-Juxta, and Johnstone, and into the adjacent areas of what used to be Peeblesshire, Selkirkshire, and Lanarkshire. In this volume I have arranged the information in chronological order.

The amount of material that is now readily available to the local historian from sources such as the internet, newspaper archives, and conventional libraries is vast and growing every day. I intend to contribute to these sources by publishing this series on the web at a point in the near future.

I hope most sincerely that readers will let me know of any errors and omissions and make suggestions for additions.

Jim Storrar
(jimstorrar@hotmail.co.uk)

Introduction

Preamble

This little volume deals with the period from the first available account of a visit to Moffat, in the year 1618, until the end of the 19th Century.

Visitors are, by definition, temporary inhabitants and as such they can rarely provide deep insights into the social, cultural, and economic lives of those who remain throughout the year. However, their written accounts of Moffat provide a wealth of information on the fabric of the town: its accommodation, buildings, transport, the price of services and, of course, the weather. Their impressions are of particular value in local history because they can often provide a more objective portrait than the resident population who may have neither the time nor the inclination to commit their ideas to print and, when they do so, they often have a vested interest in promoting their own locale. This is not to say that visitors do not arrive with preconceptions and with particular ways of looking at the world.

Before the 17th Century, visitors to the area around Moffat left their impressions on the landscape rather than their impressions of the landscape.

Prehistory

The very first hominid visitors to Moffat may have arrived something approaching 500,000 years ago but absolutely no trace of them has been found. The first direct evidence of human activity in Upper Annandale is from Catharine's Hill, about 800 metres south of Poldean Farm, where small-scale human changes to the woodlands appear to have taken place at about 5,500 BC. [1] The yew longbow found at Rotten Bottom, about 2,000 metres southwest of White Coombe, and dated to 4,040-3,640 BC gives us a glimpse of the Mesolithic hunter-gatherers of that time.

There are several traces in the Moffat area of occupation in the Neolithic (4,000 to 2,000 BC). For example, Mr. Reid ploughed up a small much-bleached Neolithic stone axe on Hunterheck Farm in about 1953 and another stone axe was found in 1982 on Whiteside Hill to the north of Kinnelhead. One of the few recognisably Neolithic monuments in the Moffat area is the long cairn at Stidriggs, about 4 kilometres south of Kinnelhead.

1

Printed in the United Kingdom
by Lightning Source UK Ltd.
102294UKS00002B/10

Moffat Place-Names

Place-names often reflect people's impressions of the landscape. Many place-names in the Moffat area derive from its geographical position and its history in relation to Gaelic, Norse, English and Welsh influences.

The origin of the name of Moffat has several possibilities including: a) Moorfoot, b) Welsh: *Maf* "that breaks out , or forms into a cluster", and *ffettan* "a sack, a bag": a plain bulging out like a sack, c) Gaelic: *Magh fada*, the "long plain", and d) Pictish Gaelic: *Magh ubh at* (pronounced Moo-uv-at), "the level area below the hill at the point formed by the waters".

Here are some possibilities that have been put forward for other local names:

Gaelic

Birnock Water	*braonagh,* "little oozy one"
Dumcrieff	*dùn* "hill" and *craoibhe* "of the tree"
Ericstane	*clach na h-éirce,* "stone of the atonement" or *clach na eireachta,* "stone of the assembly"
Loch Skene	*sgine* "of the knife" (from its resemblance to a knife cut)
Polmoodie	*poll* "stream" and *madaidh* "of the dog or wolf"
Beattock	*battock* "between two burns" or *biodach* "sharp-topped hills"
Wamphray	*uamh-fri* "den (or cave) in the forest" or *uamh aifrionn* "cave of the chapel"
Auchen Castle	*achad na caise* " the field of the stream of water, or steepness"
Grey Mare's Tail	*greith mear eas tadh ail* "the glistening cascade gushing forth from the rocky ledge"

Norse

Capelgill:	*kapilla* "chapel"
Hartfell	*hjarta* "a stag" and *fjall* "a hill" or *H-art feathal,* "the prominent great rocky mountain"
Howslack	*hol* "a hollow" and *slakki* "a shallow valley"
Meikleholm:	*mikil* "great, big" and *holmr* "low land by river"
Swatte Fell	*swaith* "bare, rocky ground" and *fjall* "a hill"

Old English

Bodesbeck	*becc,* "a stream" plus a personal name
Gallow Hill	*gealga* "gallows"
Sailfoot	*sealh* "willow"
Stot Knowe	*stot* "a horse or bullock"
Loch of the Lowes	*hloes* or *lows* "hills"

Welsh

Carrifran	*caer y fran* "raven's fort"
Evan Water	*afon* "a river"

Some names are more modern and originate from their Covenanting associations in the 17th Century. Examples include Priest Craig, Preach Hill Bog, Dob's Linn, Donald's Cleuch, and Watch Knowe.

In the Moffat area there is a limited amount of evidence of settlement in the Bronze Age (2,000 - 750 BC). One of the reasons for this may be that the area has been subject to intensive cultivation and forestation in recent years. The main archaeological remains are cairns and features known as "burnt mounds".

The Iron Age began in about 750 BC and in Scotland it is commonly considered to extend to the start of the Norse invasions in about AD 794. In the vicinity of Moffat the centre of population during this period was probably on and around Beattock Hill where the landscape is studded with the remains of settlement.

The Romans

In AD 71 or AD 72 it is likely that the legions of Petillius Cerialis, the Roman Governor of Britain at that time, penetrated as far north as Milton, three miles to the south of Moffat, and gained a fairly high level of control over the inhabitants of southern Scotland. Unfortunately there is no record of what these visitors thought of the area or of its inhabitants.

The first documentary evidence of Roman impressions of Southern Scotland is for the year AD 79. For this we are indebted to Cornelius Tacitus, the Roman historian and the son-in-law of Agricola who was then Governor of Britain. The accuracy of Tacitus's sometimes inflated accounts of his father-in-law's exploits have to be treated with caution. However, many of his statements reflected prevailing views. For example:

> "Who the first inhabitants of Britain were, whether natives or immigrants, is open to question: one must remember we are dealing with barbarians ...... The weather is foul with incessant rain and fog." [2]

When Agricola reached the Solway he found that on the other side of it dwelt the Selgovae. We cannot be sure but it is possible that members of the Selgovae populated the Moffat area before, and at the time of, the Roman occupation. A further tribe has recently come to light: the Anavionenses, a sept of the Brigantes, who may have lived along the banks of the Anava, or Annan. Their centre was probably at Burnswark to the south of Lockerbie. This evidence comes from a set of postcard-sized Roman wood tablets from the Roman settlement of Vindolanda (near Hexham). The tablets date from the late 1st and 2nd Centuries. One tablet describes a recruitment drive to persuade members of the Anavionenses to join the army and there is a disparaging reference to their fighting capabilities. [3]

The process of Romanisation (and the Moffat area would have been no exception) involved the replacement of undesirable local rulers by approved local native leaders. The formal dealings of the Romans would have been with the local elite and the population at large would have been affected only by issues such as taxation and conscription.

The Roman legacies of greatest importance to the Moffat area are: the Roman road; the complex of forts and camps at Milton; the group of five marching camps to the south and south-east of Beattock; and the signal station at White Type immediately to the south of Ericstane Hill.

The Romans finally abandoned Southern Scotland in AD 367.

After the Romans

The Dark Ages is a name given by some to the centuries after the Roman period. It is difficult to determine what happened within this period so far as settlement, farming, and social and economic development are concerned. It seems that people stopped using and making pottery, ceased producing and using coins, and built in wood rather than stone. The history of Moffat during this period is similarly "dark" and there is little evidence on which to base a picture of the lives of people in the area at this time. A period of domination by the Angles of Northumbria was brought to an end by the Viking invasions in the 9th Century and the Moffat area may then have come under the control of the British kingdom of Cumbria, also known as Strathclyde.

A legend that has been studied more than most is that of King Arthur's Myrddin (Merlin) who is said to have retreated to the Moffat area after the Battle of Arderydd in 573. Grieved by the slaying of his Lord Gwenddolau, he went mad and spent the remaining years of his life on the slopes of the Black Mountain. Nikolai Tolstoy, a descendant of Leo Tolstoy, [4] suggests that Hartfell was the Black Mountain of Arthurian legend and that Hartfell was home to Myrddin, the wise councillor and mentor of King Arthur.

Signs of Arthurian presence can be found in local place names: Arthur's Seat is the most obvious, while Merlin's Cave can be found just below the ridge.

"Ten years and forty, the sport of lawless ones,
Have I been wandering amongst sprites,
After wealth in abundance and entertaining minstrels,
After suffering from disease and despair in the forest of Caledon." [5] [6]

By 1034 we can begin to speak of the kingdom of Scotland, and picture it as having virtually the border which exists today. Moffat's history was then closely tied to the joint efforts of David I of Scotland and Henry I of England to secure the southern and northern parts of their respective kingdoms. Robert de Brus, a Norman, became a companion-in-arms to Prince David, later David I of Scotland, and followed him when he went north to regain his kingdom in 1124. The de Brus family took its name from Bruis or Brix, the site of a former Norman castle between Cherbourg and Valognes in Normandy.

One of David's first acts as King was to install Robert de Brus as Lord of Annandale in 1124. At this time, the lands of Annandale were called "Estra-Hanet", a corruption of the Welsh Ystrad Annant (the vale of the Annan). The lordship was given to Brus on feudal terms; he was to hold it by the sword and render in return military service to his king. The main purposes of the lordship were to contain the Galwegians of Nithsdale and to secure the route into Clydesdale. To help him to fulfil these conditions, Brus brought with him many Norman followers, some of whom founded families in the area. However, this does not mean that Brus drove out the previous holders of land. For example, the Kirkpatricks probably belonged to the older Scots-Irish or Scots-Saxon population while the Johnstones were also probably older residents of Annandale.

Without wishing to perpetuate the myths of William Wallace, it is worth recalling his activities in the Moffat area, based upon the text in Blind Harry's poem. [7] Soon after Christmas 1296 Wallace rode with his friends Adam Wallace, Kerly, Patrick Auchinleck and Robert Boyd to Corehead where they rendezvoused with Edward Little, Thomas Halliday, and the cleric John Blair. These early visitors were on their way to take Lochmaben Castle.

Perhaps the least welcome visitors to southern Scotland in all of its history were the armies of Edward I whose repeated invasions turned the area into an almost permanent war zone. However Annandale avoided much of this conflict because, by 1302, Bruce had bought immunity by submission to Edward.

On 15th December 1332, history provides us with another list of early visitors to Moffat. On that day Archibald Lord Douglas, William Douglas (Knight of Liddesdale), John Randolph (Earl of Moray), and Simon Fraser rendezvoused at Moffat with about a thousand horse. They were on their way to rout

Edward Baliol's army at Annan but, like Wallace's party before them, they had neither the time nor the desire to record their impressions of Moffat.

Any journey to Moffat, save the very shortest, before the 17th Century was expensive, extremely difficult and perilous, and would rarely have been undertaken except in the context of war and conflict. The taking of pleasure in travel, or travelling for the sake of travel and writing about it, is a relatively new concept and was virtually unknown until the 14th or 15th Century.

The 17th Century

Roads did not exist in Upper Annandale in the 17th Century. Agricultural produce left the farm on the hoof, following drove roads or rough tracks which were often difficult to walk and certainly not suitable for wheeled vehicles. From Edinburgh, the main track to Annandale led down the notoriously hazardous Ericstane Brae, through Moffat, and past Dumcrieff to Wamphray. The track from Glasgow came via Little Clyde and Raecleugh Rig to join the Edinburgh track just south of Annanhead Moss. Before St. Anns Bridge was built the road from Moffat to Dumfries was through Johnstone parish to Lochmaben and thence by Torthorwald and Tinwald Kirk. Another track, from Nithsdale, came to Moffat via Middlegill and the Chapel Hill.

It had been widely believed since before the 16th Century in Scotland, and elsewhere in Europe, that wells and springs had power to heal. The existence of the "queer-smelling water" at Moffat Well must have been known for a very long time to farmers, shepherds and others, including fishermen, who knew the Birnock Water.

The discovery of the medicinal value of the Well, in 1632 or 1633, has traditionally been ascribed to Rachel Whyteford. However, Matthew Mackaile suggests a later date for the discovery and ascribes it to an unnamed invalid who was accustomed to making annual visits to the wells at Brampton. While travelling through Moffat, in about 1653, he discovered a similar smell to that of the Brampton wells. The invalid discoverer of the well recommended it to his friends, and in the course of six months all sorts of sick persons resorted to it from all parts of the country. [5]

The analysis of the water provided by Matthew Mackaile's Latin tract of 1659 and the translation, much enlarged, of 1664 brought the town to the attention of a wider audience.[8] Mackaile attributed the quality of the waters to bird droppings which dissolved on the surface and found their way in solution to the source of the Well. Despite this unappealing analysis, Moffat was now firmly established as a health resort, much patronized by the legal and landed profession during the summer vacation of the law courts at Edinburgh. [9]

The 18th Century

Until the Act of Union in 1707 Scotland was possibly the poorest country in Western Europe but in the following 100 years or so, a period known as the Scottish Enlightenment, there were a remarkable series of advances in fields as diverse as philosophy and agriculture, poetry and medicine. Moffat played its part, hosting some of the key personalities of the Enlightenment; offering its waters for a series of chemical and medical analyses; and, from 1760, it was close to the forefront of the agricultural revolution.

The state of the roads in the earlier part of the 18th Century was little better than before. Even in 1770, a carrier from Selkirk to Edinburgh took a fortnight for the round trip, carrying a load of six hundred-weight at a time, and this journey was impossible in winter.[10] The Turnpike Act of 1751 provided the opportunity to dramatically improve the quality of roads, by enabling the income from tolls to be used for construction and maintenance. In about 1774, attempts were made to improve what is now the Old Carlisle Road, and Ericstane Brae was also improved and turnpiked to carry an increasing amount of light wheeled traffic. Another new turnpike road was formed to carry traffic from Glasgow to Carlisle via Moffat. This road followed the old route via Little Clyde and Raecleugh Rig and it had a great impact on Moffat. Then in 1783 money, most of it from the Earl of Hopetoun was found to pay for the "New Great Road" between Dumfries and Moffat. [11]
On 7th July 1788 the first Royal Mail from London and Carlisle to Glasgow drew up at the King's Arms in Moffat and for the next 60 years it ran every day, not always through Moffat, whatever the conditions. The 405 mile journey from Glasgow to London at first took 65 hours.

Moffat's range of waters was extended by the discovery of Hartfell Spa by John Williamson in 1748. It is difficult to overestimate the importance to Moffat of the publication, in 1769, of the first edition of Dr. William Buchan's *Domestic Medicine* in which he recommended the Moffat waters for the treatment of a range of complaints including skin diseases, scrofula, rheumatism, and loss of appetite. [12] Buchan's book became a best-seller and at least 142 English language editions were eventually published, as well as being translated into every major European language.

7

The middle of the 18th Century saw the beginning of another movement, Romanticism, which was to play a very important part in the development of the tourist industry in Scotland. The love of natural scenery for its own sake was previously a largely unfelt emotion but there was now a new appreciation of the value of scenery which was developed through the arts, particularly poetry, novels, and landscape painting. By the time the Victorian era had dawned there was a clear view of Scotland in the public imagination. A growing nostalgia for life in the countryside grew directly from growing dissatisfaction with the squalors of urban life.

In Moffat's case the novels of Sir Walter Scott stimulated interest in the local landscapes which he described in novels such as *"Redgauntlet"*, *"Old Mortality"* and *"Guy Mannering"*, and the poem *"Marmion"*. For almost the first time we find tourists making a point of visiting places such as the Grey Mare's Tail, Loch Skene, and the Devil's Beef Tub.

The 19th Century

The popularity and reputation of the Moffat waters was further bolstered by the publication, in 1800, of Dr. Thomas Garnett's pamphlet on Moffat and its mineral waters. His work was incorporated later into a larger book and this ran to several reprints and was translated into German. [67] Garnett's work reached a wider audience than conventional specialist or local literature and Moffat became better known than any other spa north of the Border. On the 15th July 1826 another significant variety of water was added to Moffat's offerings when William Walker, a Moffat shopkeeper, discovered another chalybeate (a water containing or tasting of iron) at Garpol Glen.

The 19th Century saw a revolution in transport. Thomas Telford's new road from Glasgow to Carlisle down the Evan valley was fully opened by 1828 and diverted the mail and carriage traffic on to this route from Moffat. Telford's new hotel at Beattock Bridge was popular. In 1823 the new road to Edinburgh was opened along the route which is still in use today and the road over Greenhillstairs was opened about the same time.

The completion of the new road from Glasgow to Carlisle had a major impact upon Moffat's coaching trade and upon local businesses despite the fact that the town held on to the coaching trade on the Edinburgh route. Not only was the coaching trade in Moffat suffering a decline but the number of visitors to the Well was less than in earlier years and Moffat's reputation as a watering-place was beginning to wane.

One of the responses of the people of Moffat was to establish the Moffat Bath Company in 1826 and the Baths Hall, with piped water supply from the Well, was opened in 1827. In the same year a new public water supply was introduced. Over the next 20 years a number of imposing villas were built in the town, banks and other businesses were opened, and the Moffat Gas Company was formed in 1837. [13]

In the turmoil of ideas that characterised medical thinking in the first half of the 19th Century, hydrotherapy re-emerged in the 1830s as an entire medical system, exclusive of all other forms of treatment, and based upon the internal and external application of water. Dr. James Currie, the biographer of Robert Burns and resident of Dumcrieff, had published a best-selling book on hydrotherapy in 1797 [14], but it was Vincent Priessnitz, a Silesian farmer, who popularised the formal application of hydrotherapy.[15] This was a significant step on from the traditional taking of waters at places such as Moffat where the real emphasis was on curing the ills of over-consumption, accompanied by a fresh air, a good diet, and sociability. However Moffat was to make its own claim on the popularity of hydrotherapy.

On 10th September 1847 the first public train ran from Carlisle to Beattock and on 15th February 1848 the line to Glasgow from Beattock was opened. The first edition of the *Moffat Register and Annandale Observer* was published on 4th July 1857 and by 1867 the town had a new water supply and sewerage system. The Beechgrove Recreation Grounds were opened in 1870, the new Moffat Cemetery in 1872, a new sewage works was completed in 1876, the Moffat to Beattock railway opened on 2nd April 1883, and the Station Park was established in 1888.
The opening of the railway, combined with rising standards of living, had made it possible for visitors to come to Moffat in unprecedented numbers. Other factors, such as Queen Victoria's love of Scotland and the increasing unpleasantness of life in urban Britain, made Scotland an increasingly popular destination for middle-class tourists.

In 1858 Samuel Neil, the editor of the *Moffat Register,* listed the characteristics of Moffat which "give it fitness for bestowing a feeling of peace, health, contentment, and repose to those who have become the victims of no-work, unhealthy work, or over-work :

1st   The exquisite beauty of its scenery.
2nd   The salubrity of its air and the dryness of its soil.

3rd   The finely sheltered nature of its situation, its genuine sequestratedness, the amenity of its climate, and the varieties of accommodation it is capable of affording.

4th   The kindly hospitality and honesty of those who generally entertain strangers, the courtesy and amiability of the society. The true gentility, without parade, which usually prevails.

5th   The moderation of every charge, the readiness with which such comforts of life as invalids require may be procured.

6th   The Wells.

7th   The interest in their visitors evinced by the inhabitants, and the enterprise shown in providing for their wants.

8th   The facilities for public worship." [16]

The age of mass tourism had arrived and visitors poured unto Moffat. Nevertheless, Moffat's days as a prominent watering-place were numbered. In the 1840s and 1850s other towns in Scotland, such as Rothesay, Bridge of Allan, and Dunoon opened Hydropathic establishments. [17] Between 1864 and 1882 sixteen Hydropathic establishments were opened in Scotland alone, including Moffat Hydropathic itself which opened it doors on April 5th 1878. This boom was quickly followed, in the 1880s, by bust. Supply had greatly exceeded demand and most of the new establishments faced severe financial problems and worse. Moffat Hydropathic went into liquidation in 1886, was sold by the liquidator for £25,000 in 1887, and again went into liquidation in 1899 despite taking at that time about 25,000 visitors per annum. The Hydro managed to survive before being destroyed by fire in 1921, very soon after its directors had unsuccessfully offered it to Glasgow Corporation as a sanatorium for tuberculosis patients.[18] Some of the hydropathics, including Peebles, survived through placing more emphasis upon catering for general tourism and not just medical tourism.

Moffat's consistent asset from the 17th Century to the 19th Centuries had been its mineral waters and its consequent attraction as a centre of medical tourism. Now the value of the waters was compromised both by advances in medical science and by the greater attractions of other tourist centres, including spa centres such as Harrogate and Scarborough in England; and Baden-Baden, Spa, Mentone and Marienbad in Europe. Moffat's competitors were able to offer a range of facilities and entertainments that Moffat was unable to contemplate. As early as 1822 the Rev. W. M. Wade had argued that what held Scottish watering places of all kinds back, and Moffat was no exception, was that their respectability made them dull. Unlike their English and European counterparts, they had no wish to cater for "the opulent and dissipated". [19]

The completion of the Caledonian Railway had breathed new life into Moffat but by the late 1870s there were other anxieties. Just as the railway had brought people to Moffat so it took them to other resorts and there was a growing enthusiasm for seaside holidays. The opening of the Moffat Hydro and of the Moffat to Beattock railway were, with the benefit of hindsight, too little and too late. Decline was only hastened by the economic depression of the late 1880s.

By 1896 the Moffat Baths Company found itself in deep financial trouble, both because of the calls of shareholders and the heavy burden of loan interest. In February 1897 the Moffat Commissioners agreed in principle to buy the Baths Hall as a town hall and baths for the people of Moffat and in June of that year a plebiscite of Moffat ratepayers confirmed the decision to buy. Out of 458 people in Moffat who were qualified to vote in the plebiscite, only 158 actually cast their vote with 113 for the purchase and 44 against.

The end of the 19th Century saw the first petrol-driven vehicle in Moffat but the motor car would not provide Moffat with a significant revival in its fortunes as a tourist centre until well after 1945.

Artefacts and Coins left by Roman Visitors

To the archaeologist, an artefact is an object made or modified for use by humans. Very few Roman artefacts have been found in the Moffat area. This may be because they have been destroyed or buried by agriculture or, more simply, that few items were left behind in the first place.

In 1787, while men were digging peats at Ericstane Brae near the Roman Road, a gold fibula was found. A fibula or "bow brooch" had an arched back to hold a bunch of cloth under it. This example is more than an ounce in weight and appears to be one half of a ring about ¾" broad and 3" wide.

The inscription on the fibula refers to the Vicennalia of Diocletian celebrated on 20ᵗʰ November AD 303, and this suggests that it may have formed part of the insignia sent to Emperor Constantius Chlorus in Gaul, and that its loss may have been connected with his Caledonian expedition in AD 306. The brooch was probably a personal gift from Diocletian to a senior official perhaps lost while travelling in Annandale. Some have suggested that the fibula may have belonged to Constantius Chlorus himself.

The fibula is now held in the Los Angeles County Museum and a reproduction in silver gilt is held in the National Museum of Scotland in Edinburgh.

A small model in the shape of a dolphin was found by use of a metal detector at Milton in 1982. This item is now in Dumfries Museum.

During his excavation of the Antonine fortlet at Milton in 1938 the archaeologist John Clarke found an *as* (the smallest denomination of Roman coinage) of Vespasian (69-96 AD). This coin is now in the Hunterian Museum in Glasgow.

Eleven Roman coins, nine denarii and two sestertii, were found during the 1980s in the vicinity of Milton. To the Romans a denarius was worth four times more than a sestertius. Seven of the coins from Milton are now in the Dumfries Museum while the remaining four are in the Hunterian Museum. The coins range in date from 130 BC to AD 125-128 during the reign of Hadrian.

1618 John Taylor set out to walk from London to Scotland. When he crossed the border at Carlisle he was apparently surprised to find that the sun still shone and that he could still get good ale:

> "There I saw sky above, and earth below,
> And as in England, there the sun did shew;
> The hills with sheep replete, with corn the dale,
> And many a cottage yielded good Scotch ale." [6]

John walked from Carlisle to Moffat in one day, wading the Esk and Annan "where ford was there none". At Moffat he notes:

> "My first night's lodging in Scotland was at a place called Mophat ..... I found good country entertainment, my fare and my lodgings were sweet and good, and might have fared a far better man than myself, although myself have had many times better" [20]

1633 This year (or it may have been 1632) proved to be very significant for Moffat's future. Dr. Walter Whyteford (or Whitford) had been minister at Moffat until 1620 when he moved to Glasgow before being appointed Bishop of Brechin in 1634. [21] One of Walter's daughters, Rachel, came back to visit Moffat in 1632 and the following describes her discovery. This account gives the date of discovery as 1632 rather than the widely accepted date of 1633:

> "The virtue of this water was discovered by Miss Whyteford, daughter of Bishop Whyteford, in 1632. She was married in 1633. She had been abroad, and all over England, drinking mineral waters for the recovery of her health, but found little benefit, till by accident she tasted these waters in her neighbourhood, and finding they resembled those she had used elsewhere, made a trial of them, and was cured of all her disorders.
>
> Upon this she recommended the use of them to others, and employed workmen to clear the ground above the springs

Drove Roads

From the early 17th Century the rearing of cattle and sheep was the mainstay of the agricultural economy in the Highlands of Scotland. With increases in the urban population in England, livestock became the main form of moveable wealth and long-distance droving to English markets developed. In 1662 about 3,000 cattle passed through Carlisle each day.

By the early 18th Century, Crieff was Scotland's most important cattle market and in 1723 30,000 cattle were sold at one great fair with many driven 500 miles south to London. English buyers would often hire the sellers to drive the stock. By 1772 Falkirk replaced Crieff as the main market for cattle from the highlands and three annual "trysts" were held there.

Dumfries was an important market for stock from Galloway and Ireland while the Lockerbie Tryst dealt with lambs and wool for southern buyers. As well as markets for the export trade there were markets and sales to meet more local needs at places such as Lanark and Moffat. Dealers also carried out private transactions without using the markets.

Drove cattle were often shoed or "cued" to protect their hooves from wear and the drove roads were generally over turf with grazing rights on either side. The drove roads can therefore be difficult to see on the ground today because they have often become overgrown. Progress to markets would have been slow, partly because of the need to stop frequently for watering and grazing to ensure that the loss of body weight was kept to a minimum.

The shortest route from Falkirk to England was by Lanark, Moffat and Carlisle and came into Annandale down Ericstane Hill. The main problems with this route, so far as the drovers were concerned, were the existence of several tolls and the need to cross several rivers. Nevertheless the route was not ignored and it may have carried as many as 30,000 black cattle each year.

To avoid the toll road between Moffat and Wamphray another drove road led from Ericstane via Meikleholmside, the Gallow Hill, Archbank, Caplegill, Bodesbeck, and then over to Fingland near Wamphray. Another alternative route was from Falkirk to Linton, then on to Peebles, Traquair, Tushielaw or Birkhill, Ettrick Head and Wamphray Water.

Some of the cattle that came through Moffat were sold on in Galloway and a drove road turned west to Nithsdale, following the route up the Crooked Road to Stanshielrig, Cauldholm, Stidriggs, and Mitchellslacks. A section of this route is still clearly visible where it branches west from the Crooked Road to Stanshielrig. Another route, from St Mary's Loch to Moffat, is followed by the Southern Upland Way from the flank of Craig Fell, down the side of the Cornal Burn, to Moffat Water.

(their overflowing having created a small morass) that the poor and rich might come and make use of the medicine, which nature had so bounteously offered to them." [22]

It is unlikely that Rachel was the first to be aware of the waters of Moffat Well but she may have been the first to benefit from them and she was probably the first with the will and resources (her family was a wealthy one) to make something of them.

1651   Charles Stuart, later to become King Charles II of England, was crowned King of Scots at Scone on 1st January 1651. In August Charles and his army of about 9,000 foot and 4,000 horse passed Moffat, where they were joined by about 300 horse belonging to the Duke of Hamilton. On 6th August, they breakfasted at Poldean Holm. In those days there was a hostelry of some note at Poldean although the proprietors could not have been used to a breakfast order of this magnitude. It is not recorded how satisfied Charles was with the fare but it must have been a hearty breakfast because he and his army managed to march to Carlisle before the day was done. They were on their way to defeat at the Battle of Worcester on 3rd September 1651.

The Rev. William Bennet, who retired early from the ministry to live with his mother in Moffat, composed these lines in memory of King Charles' visit to Poldean:

"But here, long since, a stirring scene,
Met eager looks from field and height,
When dazzling all the landscape green,
A royal army passed in sight;
Gay tartans glowed and helms were bright,
'Midst bonnets blue, for all would bring,
Back to his gather's throne in might,
Their new-crowned, covenanted King." [23]

1657   James, Earl of Hartfell, petitioned Cromwell's Council in Scotland for an allowance "for makeing the Well of Moffett convenient and secure by raiseing a font and walls about the said well." On 20th August, General George Monck ordered that the Earl should be permitted to use twenty-five pounds from vacant stipends for this purpose. William Rosse, Commissary of Dumfries, was charged with supervising the works, which were to be completed by 1st May 1658. [24]

1660   Lady Mary Scott, Countess of Buccleuch, who was then only thirteen years of age, had already been suffering from poor health for a number of years. A group of ten physicians and surgeons met in consultation on 26th April and recommended a course of treatment, including the drinking of the Moffat waters which she was to take "according to the direction of the physicians". [25]

1667   Robert Grierson, later to become Grierson of Lag and an infamous accomplice of Claverhouse, began three years of education at Moffat Grammar School where he had the services of a private tutor or "governor". Within nine years of leaving Moffat, Grierson was engaged in the persecution of the Presbyterians.

In Grierson's first year at Moffat his tutor was John McGowne who sent receipts to James Grierson, Robert's father, and his uncle for the sum of £100 "for fees due to me for my year's service to the aforesaid laird." The full list of chargeable items is long and includes the cost of visits to Coreheads and Brekinside, and "drink money" for the men who brought clean linen from Grierson's home at Dalscairth near Dumfries.

The items which catch the eye reflect the atmosphere in which the education of the elite was carried on in those days. Cock fighting was then a traditional activity on Fastern's Eve (Shrove Tuesday) and the "Candlemas bleis" was a gift to the master, much of which would be spent on merry-making. The thirteen-year-old Grierson must have had a good time in Moffat, albeit a little hazy at times:

	£	s	d
12/- of expenses with 1 lib 4/- of drink-money at the baptism of the school-master's son	1	16	0
for Tobacco and Pypes spent in the Chamber	3	4	0
for his Candlemas bleis, by order of the Tutor	12	0	0
for two cocks for fighting at fastern's even		8	0
left of drink-money, by the Tutor's order, when he and I went to clear our quarter at Moffat	2	18	0 [26]

1667   George Sinclair, Professor of Philosophy at Glasgow University, visited Hartfell where he measured its height with the use of a barometer. Hartfell was the first hill in Scotland to be measured in this way. [27]

1668 John Wilkie, a former minister from Twynam in Kirkcudbrightshire and a staunch Presbyterian, was held in prison in Edinburgh. In September he was in poor health and he successfully petitioned the Privy Council that his confinement should be limited to Moffat and ten miles around it. John does not say anything about Moffat itself but the following year he says this about his journey:

> "... well I know that this last summer I rode to Moffat-well, with no less than the hazard of my life; and for the present I am neither able to sit on horse nor walk on foot. [28]

1678 On 28th December John Graham of Claverhouse 1st Viscount of Dundee, also known to his friends as "Bonnie Dundee" and to his enemies as "Bluidy Clavers", was staying in Moffat. He was definitely not impressed with the behaviour of the people of the Moffat area but then he did arrive with some prejudices. In a letter to the Earl of Linlithgow he is seeking orders to unleash his dragoons:

> "My Lord, - I came here last night with the troops and am just going to Dumfries, where I resort to quarter the whole troop. I have not heard anything of the dragoons, though it be now about nine o'clock, and they should have been here last night according to your lordship's orders. I suppose they must have taken some other route.

> I am informed since I came that this country has been very loose. On Tuesday was eight-days, and Sunday, there were great field conventicles just by here, with great contempt of the regular clergy, who complain extremely when I tell them I have no orders to apprehend anyone for past misdemeanours; and besides that, all the particular orders I have, being contained in that order of quartering, every place where we quarter must see them, which makes them fear the less. I am informed, the most convenient place for quartering the dragoons will be Moffat, Lochmaben, and Annan, whereby the whole country may be kept in awe. Besides that, my Lord, they tell me that the end of the Bridge of Dumfries is in Galway, and that they may hold conventicles at our nose, [and] we not dare to dissipate them, seeing our orders confine us to Dumfries and

Inns and Hotels

The oldest known inn in Moffat is the **Black Bull** which was built as early as 1568. This may be the inn which was run by Provost Johnston in the 1720s and later in the 18th Century it was owned by James Duncan, a Moffat merchant. **Rae's Inn** was situated close to the current site of the Buccleuch Arms but on a line about 30 feet east. The Raes, hence Rae Street, were a well-known Moffat family who later emigrated to Australia. In the 19th Century a building simply called **The Hotel** may have stood where Hetherington's chemist's shop now is or it may have been just to the south of the Annandale Arms.

The **Annandale Arms** was built as the King's Arms in about 1752 by James Duncan. It was known as the "Head Inn" and was renowned as one of the most comfortable inns on the road. To the rear of the hotel was a cow shed and stabling for over 50 horses. When the Beattock to Elvanfoot road was opened in the 1820s the King's Arms lost most of its coaching traffic and the Edinburgh coaches used the Spur Inn. During the 1830s Mr. and Mrs. Cranstoun moved to the King's Arms from The Spur and gave it the new name of the Annandale Arms. Jane Cranstoun was famed for her lavender-scented sheets, her choice cooking, and her fine wines.

The **Balmoral** was built about 1764 as The Spur. William and Jane Cranstoun ran the hotel until they moved to the King's Arms in 1838. The Spur was then a private house and boarding house, Proudfoot House, before George Cavers turned it into a Temperance Hotel. In 1931 it underwent extensive alterations and was renamed "The Balmoral".

The **Buccleuch Arms** was built about 1760 but was not known as the Buccleuch until after 1860. Jane Cranstoun bought it in 1848, adding a third storey. She moved there in 1863 when she sold the Annandale Arms to Robert Norris.

The **Star** stands on the site of the Star Inn which in 1697 was part of the Provost merkland. In the latter part of the 18th Century the Star Inn belonged to Dr. James Johnstone who sold it to Samuel MacMillan, a Moffat merchant. At this time the Star was occupied by James Rae, postmaster. The Star changed hands several times until James Lumsden Brown, a baker, bought it for £710 in 1854. The current Star Hotel, designed by architect William Notman, was built in 1860.

Moffat House, built in the 1760s, did not become a hotel until 1950.

Apart from Cavers' Temperance Hotel, there were at least three other temperance establishments in Moffat. The **Harthope Temperance House** was opened in 1861 with a bequest from Johnstone of Harthope. The **Hope House Temperance Hotel** was run during the 1870s by Mrs. Cowan in Well Street. In December 1878 the **Anchor Inn** opened in Dickson Street under the auspices of Miss Shaw Stewart and Mr. Mitchell Carruthers. The Anchor offered tea, coffee, and a reading room and it was managed by Elizabeth Whyte in 1881.

Annandale. Such an insult would not please me. And on the other hand, I am unwilling to exceed orders; so that I expect orders from your Lordship how to carry in such cases, etc. etc." [28]

1679 By 7ᵗʰ January Claverhouse was in Dumfries but he had received news that the behaviour of his dragoons in Moffat had upset the local inhabitants:

"The Stewart-Depute, before good company, told me, that several people about Moffat were resolved to make a complaint to the Council against the dragoons for taking free-quarters; that if they would but pay their horse-corn and their ale, they should have all the rest free; .... I begged them to forbear till the Captain and I should come there, when they should be redressed in every thing." [28]

1682 On 17ᵗʰ April, Claverhouse was back in Moffat from where he wrote to Queensberry:

"All things are here as I would wish, in perfect peace and very regular .... For this country now is in perfect peace; all who were in the rebellion are either seized, gone out of the country, or treating their peace; and they have already so conformed, as to going to the Church, that it is beyond my expectation." [29]

1683 Sir Robert Sibbald published a short description of the sulphureous wells at Moffat in his *Nuncius Scoto-Britannus*. Robert gave away most of the copies of his book as presents to his friends so the details of his description have proved to be very elusive. [30]

1690 John Stevenson, a land-labourer from Carrick in Ayrshire first came to Moffat to seek a cure for scrofula (tuberculosis of the lymph nodes in the neck):

"I went and, in a close dependence on God, did drink of the water, and washed my wounds therewith, for the space of forty and eight hours, at proper seasons; and the Lord by this brought my hand back to the joint, and made it strong as aforetime, so that I came home with joy, and was able to go about my work. I went three summers, and stayed about six days every time at Moffat; and as my hand was restored to its place and strength the first time I went, so the following seasons I was perfectly recovered, and all my sores dried up, and my wounds healed, and I restored to a sound and healthy constitution." [31]

1690   The physician William Clerk reported on the fate of a lady who had been sent to Moffat to seek a cure for her condition. We may wonder why so many believed in the efficacy of the waters but, in the absence of alternative and effective medical treatments for conditions such as kidney stones and gallstones, it is not surprising that Moffat was a magnet for those in pain and distress:

"A Lady who had been drinking the Waters at Moffet-Wells in Annandale, Scotland, by advice of her Physicians, for a continual Vomiting, and the *Dolor Nephriticus* (kidney pain), died there in a fit of vomiting." [32]

Goats

The drinking of goats' milk was a recognised part of the treatment for those visiting Moffat to drink the waters. The combination of the water and the goats' milk was deemed to be more effective. In 1758 Dr. James Hunter, a physician practising in Moffat, leased the farms of Archbank and Clarefoot (now part of the present Archbank Farm) where he kept a flock of goats. The milk was sent to the town every morning and evening or it could be bought at the farmhouse from 1st June to the end of August. As late as 1845 it was noted that goats' whey was available in abundance in Moffat.

During the agricultural improvements in the late 18th and early 19th century, and the growth in sheep farming, many Moffat goats escaped and became feral. The decline of the popularity of the Well may have been a contributory factor. Perhaps the goats of Moffat Water are descendants of Dr. Hunter's.

Feral goats have been present in the Moffat Hills since at least 1910 and probably much earlier. The total population in the Moffat Hills was 80-112 in the period 1978-80 (censuses in October), but by 1992 it had risen to about 184, in spite of at least two large-scale removals of goats by the Hill Farming Research Organisation. There are some indications that numbers in 1999 were even higher.

Moffat in about 1780

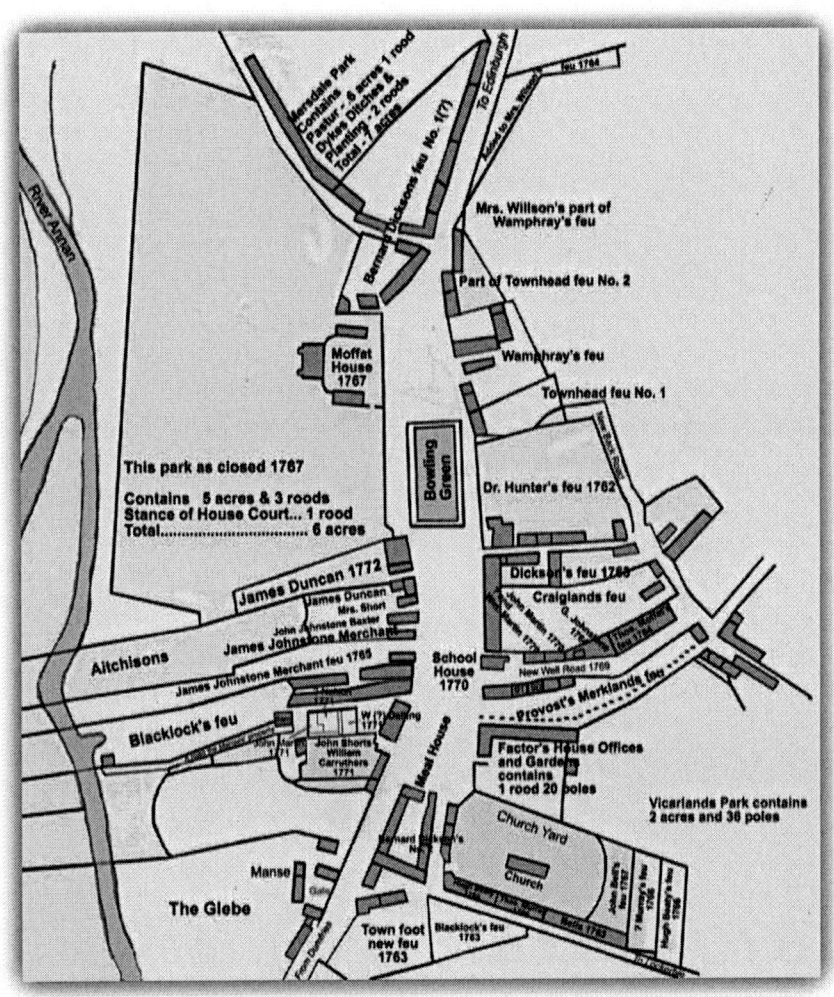

Adapted from a tracing by John T. Johnstone
from the original survey drawing of about 1780.
© National Library of Scotland

21

The Devil Drink

Throughout history many Moffat people have shown a fondness for alcoholic drink. By the time the Romans had arrived the locals were already enjoying fermented grain-based brews made from such ingredients as corn weed ("darnel") or coarse barley ("bigg"), flavoured with heather shoots, rowan berries and bog myrtle. Other native plants used for bittering in early Scottish beers were gorse and broom, plants known to intoxicate the sheep that ate their green tips and yellow flowers. Wormwood was also used and was prized for its hallucinogenic properties. Heather, which plays host to a fungus known as ergot, the precursor of LSD, probably gave ale very similar side effects.

Ingredients such as onions, wood pulp, and chicken entrails would often end up in the beer. Apart from the dubious quality of these concoctions, the results were often harmful and the government intervened. In the 15th Century, it was decreed that beer should be brewed only from malted cereals, water, yeast and hops. The superior quality of these beers won over drinkers.

Ale was churned out in the farms, taverns and houses of Moffat. Brewing followed a seasonal programme as, without adequate refrigeration techniques, beer could only be made successfully in the colder months between October and March. As early as the 14th Century brew-houses, maltkilns and "yill selling" (ale selling) are mentioned in Moffat.

Some of the old wells and springs of Moffat were apparently very good for brewing. There were two sources at Larchhill, of which the lower spring was particularly good, another at Greenbank near Birnock Water, and one at the foot of the town near the Black Bull.

In 1795, 20 licenses were issued for the sale of alcohol in Moffat. Some of these were for premises, owned by innkeepers and vintners, where one would expect to find a welcome glass. Other licenses were granted to John Murray, shoemaker; Robert Russell, watchmaker; and John Lowe, gardener.

During the 18th Century tax on malt was raised progressively. This meant that the price of ale became relatively high and increasingly out of the reach of the common man. Whisky became the more attractive drink and the Rev. Bryce Johnston, who may have had an interest in overstating his case, observed in his *General View of the Agriculture of the County of Dumfries* (1794) that:

> "These spirits, hot, fiery, new from the still, in a poisonous state, are used by them (the lower ranks) to great excess, intoxication, and the destruction of everything valuable; many have been killed by them in the very act of drinking, almost as quickly as they would have been by a dose of arsenic. "

The 18th Century

1700 An Englishman wrote to the *Scots Magazine* that he had stayed all night at Moffat and the next day he travelled south by Pudeen (Poldean) before dining at a good Scotch house at Annanholm, Wamphray. [33]

1704 An unknown traveller made a fleeting visit to Moffat:

"... and so this 17th of April 1704, I got to Moffat. This is a small straggling town among high hills, and is the town of their wells. In summer time people comme here to drink waters, but what sort of people they are, or where they get lodgings, I can't tell, for I did not like their lodgings well enough to go to bedd, but got such at I could to refresh me, and so came away." [34]

1705 Joseph Taylor journeyed from Edinburgh to London with two companions and he was less impressed than his earlier namesake. He described Moffat as "a knot of hovels":

"About two miles off Moffat, we met a great company of Scotchmen with their cloaks and caps, which made us wonder at the reason for it, in so late an hour as two at night, but upon enquiry found they had been at a funeral, it being the Scotch custom for all the country to come in on such occasions. At last we arriv'd at Moffat.

We here met with good wine, and some mutton pretty well drest; but looking into our beds, found there was no lying in them, so we kept on our cloaths all night and enjoyed ourselves by a good fire, making often protestations never to come into that country again." [35]

1710 John Simson, Professor of Divinity at Glasgow University, and James Webster, minister of the Tolbooth Church in Edinburgh, spent some time taking the waters in Moffat. Unfortunately we have no idea of what they thought of the town because they were too busy arguing their opposing views on Church of Scotland orthodoxy. In the short run it seems that Simson lost the argument because in 1729 he was suspended from all ecclesiastical functions by the Church of Scotland Assembly. However his secessionist views on patronage (the appointment of ministers by local landowners) eventually led to the creation of the Free Church of Scotland in 1843. [36]

1714 James Hart travelled from Carlisle to Edinburgh and on 8th January he stayed a night in Moffat. James does not say a great deal about Moffat but we know that he stayed at Thomas Graham's and that he paid 3s 8d for one night's accommodation for himself and his horse. [37] Thomas Graham's house may have been the building which was known as "The Hotel" which is believed to have stood a little south of the Annandale Arms. [38]

1715 The major Jacobite Risings were termed the Jacobite Rebellions by the government of the time. The first rebellion sought to restore James II's son, James Francis Edward Stuart (the Chevalier St. George), to the throne as James VIII. There was some limited sympathy for the Jacobite cause in the Moffat area because the idea of losing the "auld Stewarts" for ever was not a pleasant one. The Laird of Wamphray had some leanings to the cause but the Marquis of Annandale and the Laird of Corehead were politically more pragmatic. William Gordon, sixth Viscount of Kenmure, was commander in chief of the Chevalier's forces in the South West of Scotland.

On 11th October William Calderwood, formerly an officer in the Dutch service, who had been enlisted in the Jacobite cause by Lord Kenmure, and appointed Quarter-Master, appeared at Moffat with about seventy horse. Lord Wintoun of Carnwath is said to have joined him on that day. One suspects that they were all rather unwelcome visitors to the town.

On 12th October Kenmure joined Calderwood at Moffat having, near Lochmaben, seized some arms belonging to the militia. Their total number was then about 150 horse. Kenmure set up the standard of the Chevalier at Mar's Dale or Mearsdale. The standard was made, for this occasion, by Lady Kenmure, the sister of Robert, sixth Earl of Carnwath. It was very handsome; one side being blue, with the arms of Scotland wrought in gold; on the other side a thistle with the words *No Union* wrought underneath the thistle. Above it were the words *Nemo Me Impune Lacessit*. White pendants were attached to the standard, on which was inscribed - *For our Wronged King and Oppressed Country! For our Lives and Liberties!*

24

At about midnight on 13ᵗʰ October, the insurgents left Moffat to march towards Dumfries with the intention to surprise the town but on hearing of the strong preparations which had been made to receive them they agreed, after many disputes and contentions among themselves, to march to Lochmaben.

Kenmure's forces went on to join other Jacobites from the Highlands and the North of England but they met their end between the 9ᵗʰ and 14ᵗʰ of November at the Battle of Preston. Meanwhile the Earl of Mar was unable to defeat government forces in Scotland and he fled to France with James Francis Stuart. Kenmure was beheaded on Tower Hill, London on 24ᵗʰ February 1716. [39] [40]

1717 William Laidlaw was James Hogg's maternal grandfather. He was usually known as Will O'Phaup after the farm (Phawhope, at the head of the Ettrick Valley) where he was a shepherd for fifty-five years. For feats of frolic, strength and agility he had no equal in his day. He was also known for his sense of humour, his ability to converse with fairies, and his fondness for good black French brandy in times when the price of whisky was beyond the means of most. In about this year he made one of his frequent visits to Moffat:

> "Many a hard bouse he had about Moffat, and many a race he ran, generally for wagers of so many pints of brandy; and in all his life he never was beat. He once ran at Moffat for a wager of five guineas, which one of the chiefs of the Johnstones betted on his head. His opponent was a celebrated runner from Crawford-Muir, of the name of Blaikley, on whose head, or rather on whose feet, a Captain Douglas had wagered. Will knew nothing of the match until he went to Moffat, and was very averse to it. "No that I was ony fear'd for the chap," he said; "but I had on ma ilka-day claes, and as mony leddies and gentleman war to be there to see the race, I didna like to appear afore them like an assie whalp."

> However, he was urged, and obliged to go out and strip; and, as he told it "a poor figure I made beside the chield wi' his grand ruffled sark. I was sae affrontit at thinking that Will O'Phaup should hae made sic a dirty shabby appearance afore sae mony girt folks and bonny leddies, that not a fit could rin mair nor I had been a diker. The race was down on

25

Annan-side, and jimply a mile, out and in; and, at the very first, the man wi' the ruffled sark flew off like a hare, and left me to come waughling up ahint him like a singit cur, wi' his din sark and cloutit breeks. I had neither heart nor power, till a very queer accident befell me; for Scots grund! Disna the tying o' my cloutit breeks brek loose, and in a moment they were at my heels, and there I was standing like a hapshekel'd staig! "Off wi' them Phaup! Off wi' them!" cries ane. Od, sir, I just sprang out o' them; and that instant I fand my spirits rise to the proper pitch.

The chield was clean afore me, but I fand that if he were a yeagle I wad o'ertak him, for I scarcely kenn'd whether I was touching the grund or fleeing in the air. I got by him, but I had not muckle to brag o', for he keepit the step on me till within a gunshot o' the starting point."

Will never went to Moffat, that the farmers did not get him in their company, and then never did he get home to Phaup sober. There was one time in Moffat, that he was taken in, and had to pay a dinner and drink for a whole large party of gentlemen. This was probably for a wager. He had not only to part with all his money, but had to pawn his whole stock of sheep. He then came home with a heavy heart, told his wife what he had done, and that he was a ruined man. She said that since he had saved the cow, they would do well enough. The money was repaid afterwards, so that Will did not actually lose his stock; but after that he went seldomer to Moffat. [41]

1723 John Macky visited Moffat and wrote in a letter to his friend abroad:

"Annandale is within the shire of Dumfries, adjoin to Nithsdale: it's but a coarse moorish country, chiefly inhabited by the name of Johnstone, of which the Marquis of Annandale is chief: His chief seat in this country is Lockhead (*sic*), near the famous Wells of Moffat that purge like those of Scarborough, and are much frequented; but here is no raffling *(gambling)*, walking and dancing, as at Bath and Tunbridge: an universal quietness reigns in the place." [42]

1726 Daniel Defoe had been to Scotland on previous occasions. For example in 1706 he had been sent as an agent charged with the task of furthering parliamentary union between England and Scotland. In 1726 he visited Moffat during his tour throughout Great Britain and he provides a very graphic description of Moffat Well:

"The more remarkable medicinal fountains in Scotland are Moffat Wells, which spring from the top of a rock near the town of that name in Annandale. The wells are two in number, near one another; the higher well runs through whitish and crystalline stones, and the lower through black ones, resembling marcasites of antimony. The smell of the water is like that of gunpowder, and it dyes silver of a black colour. To the stones of the upper well grows a matter resembling stinking sulphur of antimony, of a yellowish red colour; the stones of the lower well are of a metallic antimony, and some of them contain a metallic matter, that sparkles like antimony.

Where the stream of the lower well runs down into a neighbouring brook, there sticks to the rock a whitish salt, and perhaps a nitrous matter, which has the diuretic virtue of the water. Those waters also purge by stool and vomit, and are very good against colic and nephritic pains, because they powerfully remove the obstructions of the bowels. They are outwardly applied to ulcers, and against pains in the joints; they are strongest in their operation in the driest season of the summer and autumn, but are not so good in a rainy, or in the winter-season." [43]

1727 The Rev. Thomas Boston visited Moffat to take the waters and he did not have a good experience:

"I fell under a considerable illness, which I took to be the effect of Moffat-well water, having advanced to three chopins (about 4½ pints) of it, being weary of the time the drinking of it took up. On the Thursday's night it came to an extremity, so that death stared me in the face and the sending for help proposed was delayed, till it should be seen what the morrow would produce. ... On the morrow my illness abated.." [44]

1729 George Skene journeyed on horseback from Edinburgh to London. He was accompanied by his younger brother David, an older friend named Thomas Burnett, and a servant. Their main interests on the way appear to have been the inns they stayed in, the quality of the food and drink, the landladies and, more particularly, the servant girls. The language of George's account shows a lack of delicacy which is characteristic of the period but the part in which he describes Moffat is atypically free of lewd observations. He did not intend that his notes should ever be published and this probably explains the disjointed rendition of his description.

The four began their journey on 8th September 1729 and on 9th September they left Bield, at Tweedsmuir:

" .. for five miles up Tweedside, saw not a house till we came to one called Tweed: braefoot *(Braefoot)*, because at the foot of the braes whence the Tweed rises, for nine miles from Bield, we saw not a stack of corn, the people making hay of the rough grass, for their cows and winter, and living on milk etc.

We put up at Provost Johnston's *(this may have been the Black Bull)*, a man of good sense, in Moffat, the landlady ugly to horror and an English woman eternally drunk. The well at Moffat lies a mile and three-quarters north of the town out of a rock like the shell of a kill *(perhaps kiln)*, tastes strongly of gunpowder, and bluish colour'd, is reckoned exceeding good for all the Scurvey and all scroplous diseases, it purges and they likewise bath with it, a good young buxom and willing girl was at the well filling some barrels. It yields the Spring 24 loads which is about 40 or 48 pints each hour and each load is 12 pence.

There is a very fine oblong square bowling green in the middle of the town, for the diversion of the Company which is extraordinary numerous for such a place, they enter by the barress gates (opposite to one another) level with the flat of the green, it is inclosed with a brick wall, and against the wall is thrown up round within a grass bank on ye top of which is a yew hedge round, and single yews planted and cut in shapes. Here David was sick, weary and bum-flean *(with sore buttocks from riding)* and went to bed without supper. Here we saw Coll. Francis Farquhar.

The well is good for washing sores, and especially if a right bit of the rock is taken which the water man knows, and made reed hot in a furnace and throwen in among a bottle of water is reckoned excellent for sores.

The whole victuals in this country is always mutton because they live intirely of sheep of which they take good care, haining *(enclosing)* the grass near home all summer, not allowing any cattle to dung on it which rotts the sheep, and keeping them in the far hills all summer which makes that you see but few as you come along. They will pay here for grassing and smearing one sheep 18 pence, of which the smearing is 2½ or 2 pence only. This town and well belongs to Johnstoun Marquis of Annandale where he'll have about £4,000 per annum *(James, the second Marquis of Annandale, died in Naples in 1730)*. It is a regality and he has a gallows here but poor, never having hang'd any, tho' a poor people, a poor countrey, and not a little inclin'd to stealing. There is none of the town few'd, which is a loss to the place and makes the houses few and bad.

Pay'd our bill which was 17 shillings sterling and 1 penny. We mounted half an hour after six *(on the morning of 10ᵗʰ September)*." [45]

1732 Sir John Clerk of Penicuik owned Dumcrieff at this time and it was in about this year that his grandson paid him a visit there. The grandson later recollected:

> "... the old Baronet *(Sir John)* carried some English Virtuoso to see a supposed Roman camp ; and on his exclaiming at a particular spot, "This I take to have been the Praetorium", a herdsman, who stood by, answered, "Praetorium here, Praetorium there, I made it wi' a slaughter spade."" " [46]

1733 A large part of Sir John Clerk's attraction to Moffat was the water:

"I was frequently troubled with red scorbutick *(scurvy)* spots, which continued for a month or two, unless when they happened to be removed by Moffat water. In the month of August I was with my Wife and some of my family at Drumcrief. We made use of Moffat water, each of us a Bottle at a time, and found great benefite by it, for this water contributes much to sweaten the blood." [47]

1736 The Hon. Thomas Tickell Esq., Secretary to their Excellencies the Lord Justices of Ireland, arrived at Moffat, for the benefit of the water, with his Lady and Family. [48]

1737 William Fordyce, from Culsh in Aberdeenshire, left Edinburgh for Moffat on 7th July where he stayed before leaving for Lanark on 26th July. William kept a detailed journal of his expenses for his stay in Moffat and this illustrates how expensive travel was at that time. William's bill for his 18 days in Moffat was roughly equivalent to 4 months' income at that time for a building labourer in Edinburgh:

	£	s	d
for 4 lbs. of sugar for my tea when at Moffat	1	10	0
for horse hyre from Edinburgh to Moffat	8	2	0
to the woman that keeps the well	0	12	0
for room rent from the time I came to Moffat, for myself and servant, to Mrs. Grahame. 18 nights.	6	0	0
for four baiths in same time	2	8	0
to the servant maid for her service	1	0	0
for my own and servant's diet	9	18	0
to Dr. Gravenstock for his advice, and two dozes of salts for making the water operate	6	18	0
to the poor of Moffat from the time I came	0	8	0
for shaving and dressing my wigs the time at Moffat	0	12	0
for washing Geo. Brumner's linings	0	5	6
lost in the bowling green	0	9	0
bowling green mail (rent)	0	12	0
Total	*42*	*6*	*6* [49]

1740 Sir John Clerk of Penicuik stayed at Dumcrieff with his wife and two daughters. Sir John had owned Dumcrieff from 1726 to 1737 but it was now the property of his son. Sir John's family were still regular visitors to Moffat where he took the Moffat waters to successfully treat his scorbutic spots. Another alarming disease left him by the simple expedient of ceasing to drink the juice of raw oysters. He must have felt that Dumcrieff had taken a turn for the worse because he noted:

> "My wife and I had the best room but it is ill provided with furniture and would take a folding up bed with curtains of the same colours. The dining room below stairs is not in order. Painted paper would be best to hang round it. The grass on the water side is very rich and fit for duck lands but it is in the hands of bad tenants and their cows and is good for nothing." [50]

1745 By this time, Moffat was well established as a favourite watering-place:

> "Morning is the approved time of visiting the Well and on fine mornings a visitor or two may be forward by six o'clock; but it is not till about seven that there is any decided evidence of briskness. Pedestrians then begin to stream in, and about half an hour later two or three omnibuses, and sometimes several other vehicles, add their contents to the swelling tide, and the verandah is completely animated; the company present - ladies, gentlemen and children - numbering perhaps two hundred. It is the bounden duty of one and all to drink." [51]

1745 The Rev. Dr. Alexander Carlyle noted that Dr. John Sinclair, an important figure in the development of the School of Medicine at Edinburgh University, and Sir John Clerk had both found that Moffat waters agreed with them, and they frequented it every season in their turn for a month to six weeks, "and by that means drew many of their patients there, which made it be more frequented than it has been of late years, when there is much better accommodation". [31]

Bonnie Prince Charlie had landed in Scotland in July and Alexander Carlyle goes on to say that:

The Music of Moffat

Visitors to Moffat required entertainment, to relieve the day-to-day routine of a small country town.

The first record of a musician being employed to lead the band at Moffat was when John Bruce, a gifted fiddler from Braemar, was retained in the latter half of the 18th Century. John was a Jacobite who had been imprisoned for his active support of the '45. For many years he walked from Braemar to Moffat for "the season" before he settled eventually in Dumfries.

> To hear John Bruce exert his skill,
> Ye'd never grudge anither gill :
> O ! how he scorn'd th' Italian trill,
> And variations ;
> And gart his thairm-strings speak, at will,
> True Scots vibrations!

The need to provide entertainment led to the formation, in the 1850s, of the Moffat Band Fund Committee which retained entire professional bands for the season. Funds were raised through subscriptions with about half coming from local traders and half from visitors to the town. A recurring theme in *The Moffat Register* was the appeal for money to support the band.

Over a period of 11 weeks at the height of the season the band would play at the Well every morning (weather permitting) from 7.45 to 8.45 and in front of the Baths Hall from 2.30 to 3.45 p.m. This was followed by a concert every evening (except Fridays) between 8.00 and 9.30 in the Hall. Friday evenings were reserved for promenades (formal balls) to which the admission charges in 1858 were 1/- for ladies and 1/6 for gentlemen.

One of the first bands to be retained, in 1857, was that of F.S. Bushez of Glasgow, under the direction of R.B. Stewart of the Queen's Theatre, Edinburgh. In 1858 T.H. Allwood, a noted solo violinist of the Theatre Royal, Glasgow, directed the band. The musical offerings were diverse, ranging from pieces by Rossini, Verdi and Bellini to traditional Scottish melodies such as "Bonnie Doon" and "Auld Robin Gray".

In 1858 Mr. Allwood's band comprised Mr. Kelly on flute, Mr. Calcott on piano, Mr. Hannan on trombone and violoncello, Mr. Towndross on second violin, and Mr. Harper. The cost of retaining the six-man band for 11 weeks in the summer of 1858 was £132. A Mr. Howard directed the band in 1859 which then included Messrs. Zoblinski (flute), Tyler (clarionet), and Plimmer (cornet). In 1868 the Band of the Upper Annandale Rifle Volunteers, initially led by Mr. Broadhurst, took the place of the professional bands.

"I had promised Mr. H. Bogle and his sister to pass a few days with them at Moffat …. When I got to Moffat, I found my expecting friends still there, though the news had arrived that the Chevalier Prince Charles had landed in the north with a small train, had been joined by many of the clans, and might be expected to break down into the low country, unless Sir John Cope, who was then on his march north, should meet with them and disperse them. I remained only a few days at Moffat, as the news became more important and alarming every day; and, taking leave of my friends, I got home to Prestonpans on the evening of the 12th of September." [52]

1745   On 29th July George Dalrymple, the fifth son of the first Earl of Stair, died at Moffat. No account of early visitors to Moffat would be complete without mention of his sister-in-law Eleanor Dalrymple, Countess of Stair, who became a prominent society figure in London, Bath, and Edinburgh following her marriage in 1708 to John Dalrymple, second Earl of Stair. Her annual visits to Moffat to take the waters helped to turn it into a successful spa. [53] [54]

1745   In November, the western division of Prince Charlie's army marched south via Peebles, Broughton, and Tweedsmuir to Moffat. Any visitors to the Moffat waters had long since fled the town to seek refuge in their homes and to secure their valuables. At about 1.00 p.m. on 5th November a quartermaster of the Highland Army reached Moffat where he demanded meat, drinks and quarters for 4,000 men and 600 horse. The main division of troops, with artillery and 150 cartloads of baggage, then assembled on Ericstane Brae at 9.00 a.m. on 6th November, from whence they were to march in good order to Moffat. The officers of each corps were under orders to ensure that their men were on their best behaviour and that they did not carry out any plundering and looting. [55] [56]

Unfortunately we have no record of what these "visitors" thought of Moffat. On Friday 8th November they marched via Kirkpatrick Kirk and Johnstone Kirk to Lockerbie. [57] On their way they stole a horse at Nether Murphat which was returned when a local farmer explained to the soldiers that the owner of the house was the recently-widowed mother of several children. A group of mourners at Kirkpatrick-Juxta Churchyard were less fortunate: they were most impressed when the soldiers drew up and saluted the coffin as a mark of respect, but when they came out of the churchyard after the burial they found that their best horses had been stolen. [58]

The western division of the army met with the eastern division near Carlisle and they marched south, reaching Derby on 4th December before beginning their retreat two days later. When the army was north of Carlisle it split into two columns, both heading for Glasgow: one, including Prince Charlie himself, made its way via Dumfries and Nithsdale while the other, under the command of Lord George Murray, went via Annandale, Moffat and Douglas.

The eastern column, comprised of about 2,000 men, arrived in Moffat on 21st December and they halted there for the following day. Lord George Murray had struggled for weeks through cold and wet weather and he made a note of his stop at Moffat:

> "I was next day almost cured, and the day thereafter quite free of my cold and cough. We halted a day at Moffat. It was Sunday, and having episcopal ministers along with us, we had sermon in different parts of the town, where our men all attended. Our people were very regular that way, and I remember at Derby the day we halted, as a battle was soon expected, many of our officers and people took the sacrament." [59]

Few Moffat men had joined the Highlanders. William French, the younger brother of the laird of Frenchland, took his chances with them and was captured during a skirmish at Clifton, near Penrith. He escaped and spent the rest of his life in England. Six Moffat undesirables also followed the army into England but when they returned to Moffat after the march to Derby they received a very hostile reception and the townspeople would have hung one of them, an Irishman. Having been trained in the use of the broadsword, the former soldiers threatened that "if they were molested they would kill every man, woman and child in the place and burn all the houses". The minister, Rev. David Brown, intervened and persuaded the men to leave the town. They were last seen going in the direction of Dumfries in the company of six women natives of Moffat, known to everybody as "common randies".

1746   A volunteer with the Duke of Cumberland's army passed through Moffat, probably on his way back from Culloden:

> "Moffat is but a small Town, noted for its Medicinal Well, which is situated just by the Side of a small rocky River, a Mile out of Town; it consists of two Wells, one above the other, springing out of the solid Rock; the Water tastes like rotten Eggs, or rather like the Washings of a Gun Barrel; and on the Sides of the rocky Well, I found many curious and rare Plants.
>
> The Waters are said to Purge and Vomit, and are mightily esteemed against Cholicky and nephritical Disorders, powerfully removing Obstructions in the Bowels. They are applied outwardly to Ulcers, and for Pains in the Joints; and in Summer-time here is a great Concourse of the Nobility and others from Scotland, who come to drink the Waters; and have a Ball Room, where they meet twice a Week." [60]

1746   George Milligen, Surgeon at Moffat, wrote his account of the mineral waters at Moffat Well. He provides some interesting details of when and how the waters should be taken:

> "The proper season for using them *(the waters)* is between the middle of April and the end of September; but some continue their use all winter. The time of continuing in the bath is from quarter of an hour to a whole hour or more. Such as bath the whole body usually do it twice or thrice a week in the evening.
>
> The water is commonly drunk between the hours of six and eleven in the morning. They who allow most time, and drink gradually, take the best method. None is drunk after dinner. I never prescribe more than three quarts, or a gallon at most; and this quantity but seldom. Sometimes an emetic or two, and two or three purges, should be given as preparatory medicine. The exorbitant use of purges along with the water I cannot approve of, although it is general practice here. Too strict a regimen need not to be observed. But milk, salted meat, eggs and fish, are improper food. Riding and moderate exercise assist the water.

Some have used this water for the gout, but I cannot say that I have known it do any great matters in it. But we have instances of it having done service in palsies. Two gentlemen, who were troubled with a numbness, and almost total want of feeling, with a great feebleness of all their limbs, especially the legs, after being well purged, drank the waters with salt of amber, but not every day, took a glass of bitters daily, and bathed thrice a week, using the water warm in the evening, and cold next morning; at which time they continued only a few minutes in it. One of these gentlemen was perfectly recovered, and the other became much better.

The scrophulous, after dropping the use of the water, should recommence purging and mercurial doses for some time, and persist in the use of emollient and diuretic medicines, and among these chiefly the millipedes *(an emulsion of millipedes was commonly used in medicine at this time).*" [61]

1747   Learned papers on the quality of the Moffat waters were coming thick and fast. Dr. Andrew Plummer, Professor of Chemistry at the University of Edinburgh published a paper in which he was very scathing about the quality of Matthew Mackaile's analysis of 1659. Having visited Moffat, Plummer arranged for the delivery to Edinburgh of samples of the water "in Bottles well corked and waxed about the Neck." The water was then subjected to a series of tests which included boiling, evaporation, distillation, the addition of various acids, and mixing with syrup of violets. [62]

1748   Sir John Clerk found that all was not well at the Well:

"As the well is quite open night and day there is a number of diseased scrophulous, leperous people lying about it and who seem to be watching for an opportunity to wash their sores unseen by the two keepers." [63]

1748   From the diary of an unnamed youth we learn that he was sent to Moffat to drink the water and to bathe. He was lodged in the house of one John Gillespie, and he had a furnished room. His mother came with him and saw him fairly settled before she went home again. With the use of the waters he gathered so much strength that he went to the Latin School in Moffat taught at that time by Mr. Dobie, an eminent man in his profession. However the youth found, to his astonishment and mortification, that he was a very dull scholar, and notwithstanding his application he was still of the lowest order. His retentive memory was gone.

The youth stayed at Moffat until the season began to turn cold for the drinking water, went home and returned in the spring, when he was boarded with one Robert Don, a gardener. His wife's name was Marion Henry, who was an acquaintance of both his father and mother, but she took care of herself and very little of him, as she gave such a scanty diet that he could not say he ever knew what it was like to be straightened for victuals. He had some pocket money and bought bread, and continued with Marion until he went home in the summer of 1749. [64]

1749 The Earl of Balcarres fell ill and he was advised by the family physician to travel from Fife to visit the waters at Moffat. It was there that he met Anne Dalrymple and her charms made him soon forget every pursuit but that of love. "In his brigadier wig and gouty shoe, he lost his heart to fat, fair, and severely sensible Miss Dalrymple." [65]

Anne and the Earl were soon married despite the fact that he was aged sixty while she was only twenty-two years of age. The potency of the Moffat waters may take some credit for the fact that Anne went on to bear him eight sons and three daughters. [66]

1750 In about this year William Horseburgh made several trips to Hartfell Spa, and to the River Annan, to examine the waters that had been discovered by John Williamson in 1748. He concluded that the water was of the class "aquae Martiatae" *(alkaline)* and therefore good for curing "itchy, hot, tettarous *(skin)* eruptions, old obstinate ulcers and sores", and, "it has likewise been of great service in disorders of the stomach and bowels". [63]

A typical scene in Moffat was described as follows:

"In spring there met round the little wells at Moffat a throng, in their gayest and brightest, from society in town and country, sipping the unpleasant waters, and discussing their pleasant gossip. At the bowling green were to be seen sauntering valetudinarian city clergy, men of letters, and country gentlemen, ladies of rank and fashion; while the diseased, decrepit, of the poorest rank, who had toilsomely travelled from far-off districts to taste the magic waters, loitered in their rags in the village street." [67]

1751 William Horseburgh provided a number of case studies for those who had been helped by the waters of Hartfell Spa. For example, Mrs. Scott of Edinburgh contracted a rheumatic fever in 1750, which continued for about three months, leaving her very low. In May 1751, when she visited Moffat, she had leg pains and sores and oedema in her legs. She had a poor appetite; she was very weak and did not sleep well:

"She drank the sulphureous water, a bottle a-day for a month, but rather found herself worse; she bathed ten times in the same water, warmed, and was remarkably worse by the use of the bath; whereupon she gave over the water, and drank ewe's milk whey for six weeks, a mutchkin (about 0.4 litres or 0.7 pints) every morning .... but the pains and swellings in her legs and hands remained the same. Dr. John Clerk was consulted who ordered a box of gum pills, a bottle of the sulphureous water every morning, and half a mutchkin of the Hartfell Spaw every forenoon at eleven. She then betook herself entirely to the Hartfell water, of which she drank during a month, a bottle a-day. On ten or twelve days she was quite delivered from all complaints; and has at present a good appetite, good spirits, is strong, and her flesh recruited." [68]

1752 A sickly twelve year-old James Boswell was sent to Moffat from Edinburgh by his father. In the sketch of his life which Boswell later wrote for Rousseau, he says that he had a bad cold which left him with nervous indigestion and scorbutic complaints. In another letter Boswell recounted that:

"I was weakened in body and mind, and my natural melancholy increased. I was sent to Moffat, the spa of Scotland. I was permitted a great deal of amusement. I saw many lively people. I wished to be lively myself, and insensibly regained my health, after having imagined that I should certainly be ill all my life." [69]

Even at this early age James was swiftly moved by the opposite sex and it was probably on this visit that he met a Miss Mackay with whom he fell deeply in love. [70]

Boswell later described an unpleasant experience from this visit:

"... one cannot imagine anything more consoling than after a day of annoyance and fatigue to undress and stretch one's self out at full length in fluid warmth, to have one's nerves gently relaxed, to enjoy indolent ease and forget all one's cares. I experienced a little of that enjoyment when I was at Moffat in Scotland for the mineral waters. But my pleasure was very crude because I was taking the baths for my health, and there were no conveniences for bathing for pleasure. I was put into a horrible tub, a scanty covering was thrown over me, and in that state I was obliged to remain for half an hour. I had as my supervisor a barbarian of a Presbyterian preacher, who called out from time to time in a harsh voice, "Take care, you rogue! If we see the least disobedience to our orders we shall proceed to instant punishment." And that was why I kept quiet, though I was extremely bored." [71]

It turned out that Boswell was ill throughout his life, suffering from an alarmingly wide range of complaints. He had a very good constitution, which was just as well because he was to be in great need of the best that contemporary medicine could offer him. Boswell was clearly very fond of Moffat and he referred to it in his writing:

"How easily and cleverly do I write just now! I am really pleased with myself; words come skipping to me like lambs upon Moffat Hill; and I turn my periods smoothly and imperceptibly like a skilful wheelwright turning tops in a turning-loom. There's fancy! There's simile!" [72]

1753 A party of fishermen climbed up to Loch Skene and they took a pony with them that was well loaded with food and other provisions necessary to ensure a good day out. They had a very good time and at the end of the day a David Fraser was so inebriated that he was unable to walk or, indeed, to stand. To get him back to Moffat, the others laid Fraser face down on the back of the pony. By the time the party had reached the hill above Polmoody they found that Fraser had died from suffocation. A flat stone on the hill by Fraser's Syke was inscribed: D.F. DIED D---K.[73] I wonder if the stone is still there.

1754 In about this year, William Roy completed his map of the Moffat area. The main impetus to the Roy Military Survey of Scotland was the Jacobite Rebellion of 1745-1746, when the Hanoverian military commanders in Scotland found themselves "greatly embarrassed for want of a proper Survey of the Country". [74]

Roy's map (see below) shows a number of interesting features including some early examples of enclosed land at Frenchland, Alton, south of the Holm Road, and on the southern slopes of the Gallow Hill. The farms of Barns, Quaecleugh, and Hillhouse are shown on the map but those names disappeared in 1828 when the farms were incorporated within an enlarged Chapel Farm.

By kind permission of the British Library Board © The British Library Board

1756 Three French travellers, having negotiated the temptations of Lockerbie, visited Moffat:

> "We passed through the village of Locharby, where there was no family that did not sell liqueurs along the road. About one mile from Moffat, which contains only forty or fifty extremely poor families, are the most frequented waters in the Kingdom .... Everything here is more expensive than at Bath" [75]

1756 Mrs. Calderwood and her husband made the journey to Spa in the Low Countries. In her journal, Mrs. Calderwood makes some interesting comparisons between Spa and Moffat:

> "The room-rents are cheaper than at Moffat, like about seven shillings a week for the bedrooms, and less for the smaller rooms; every house has a good low room for dining in, which they call a salle.

> They said it was the fashion over all this country for people to travel for nothing, and anybody who could not afford to go in a carriage, if they had business from one country to another, never thought of money to bear their charges, but begged everything they got; and the folks on the road had learned to think themselves obliged to feed and lodge them for nothing, just as the lasses at Moffat think themselves obliged to carry the men over the waters." [76]

1757 James Boswell was again under the thrall of melancholy and depression and he made a second visit to Moffat in that summer. He had become interested in Methodism but in Moffat came under the influence of the extraordinary character of John Williamson, who had been a sheep farmer. Williamson had discovered Hartfell Spa in 1748 and he was now wandering the countryside looking for valuable minerals and preaching the virtues of the transmigration of souls and vegetarianism. Boswell seems to have spent some time with him and whether as a result of this or simply through the passing of time his mood and health improved.

1759 In the summer of this year James MacPherson, of Ossian fame, was in Moffat as tutor to the family of Thomas Graham of Balgowan. [77]

Despite claims to the contrary, MacPherson certainly did not stay at Moffat House where construction was not started until 1762. We do not know what MacPherson thought of Moffat but he met Alexander Carlyle and John Home there. The latter, who was an annual visitor to Moffat, was not complimentary about the site of the Well but he left his explanation of its popularity in the following terms:

> "No grace did nature here bestow;
> But wise was nature's aim:
> She bade the healing waters flow,
> And straight the graces came." [78]

John Home at first astonished the people of Moffat by his habits of thinking aloud and reciting poetry as he walked around the town. He was also looked on with some suspicion as a Church of Scotland Minister who had written *Douglas*, a tragic play.

Moffat at about this time was the occasional resort of a sizeable group of men of letters including Hugh Blair, Church of Scotland minister and university professor; David Hume, philosopher and historian, who in 1745 had acted as a paid companion to George, third Marquis of Annandale; Joseph Black, chemist and physician; George Lawrie, Church of Scotland minister and patron of poetry; and Thomas Blacklock, the blind poet and writer.

1759   Henry Grey Graham, the Scottish social historian, paints a fine picture of the social life of the privileged in Moffat at this time:

> "The bowling-green at Moffat about the middle of the 18th Century was a gay scene. There were present visitors from all parts of Scotland who were glad to while away the time between the intervals of drinking the sulphur waters which had gained fame for the village. Lairds and their wives from remote districts came to the wells, anxious to join the rank and fashion which every season gathered there - "nabobs" who returned from the Indies, possessed of lacs of rupees and bilious constitutions; "Tobacco lords" from Glasgow with airs of consequence as pronounced as their accents; ministers in blue, professors in black, and lawyers in scarlet coats, with ladies in their hoops and sacques of brilliant hues." [79]

1760 A significant event in Moffat's history was the passing of an Act, in 1760, whereby the administration of the estate of the Marquis of Annandale was granted to his uncle, John Earl of Hopetoun. The Marquis, George Vanden Bempde, had been certified as a lunatic. The Earl of Hopetoun's enlightened and progressive actions did much to develop the economy of the area: [80]

> **And whereas** the Town of *Moffat*, Part of the said Ten Pound Land of *Moffat*, is greatly reforted to by Perfons of all Ranks and Conditions, for the Benefit of ufing the Mineral Waters in the Neighbourhood of the faid Town; but the faid Company have hitherto been very ill accommodated by Reafon of the Badnefs and Poornefs of the Houfes, and other Buildings in the faid Town, and by the Want of many other neceffary Conveniencies.
>
> **And whereas** many of the Houfes in the faid Towns of *Moffat* and *Annan*, belong in Property to the faid Marquis, which are all of them very poor and mean, and fallen into fuch Difrepair and Decay, that many of them are already ruinous; and moft of them muft foon be fo, if not rebuilt, which would occafion a very great Charge and Expence.

1760 In May, Richard Pococke, Bishop of Meath, came to Moffat from the south. Pococke was described by Mrs Delaney as "the dullest man that ever travelled: but he is a good man". His description of the valley is certainly a little dull and it makes it difficult to pinpoint the route he followed. However in some of his writing he is very quick to come to the point:

> "We came in between the mountains which open and make a wider vale towards the part where the river has run from the north, and begins to run east and west, and forms a pleasant romantic amphitheatre encompassed with high mountains. Moffat is a small town in this vale. It is the estate of the Marquis of Annandale, who is a lunatic, and Lord Hopton (*sic*) is the curator, who is setting on foot a manufacture of shalloons (*lightweight wool or worsted fabrics*) and serges (*durable twilled fabrics*) here.
>
> I went two measured miles to the old well, passing near a British round fort with a keep in it and in which they had dug to find treasure. From this place I crossed the

mountains towards the road to Edinburgh and .... we came to the new well called Hartfell Spaw, found out about seven years ago by Mr. Williamson the Pythagorean, who eats nothing that causes the destruction of an animal, occasioned by his compassion for the game he saw dying when he was about eighteen years old. This spaw is on the Duke of Queensborough's (*sic*) estate, who has made a good carriage road to it .... On the other side of the rivulet, lower down, are copper mines. They belong to Mr. Grampton (*a muddled reference to the estate of Granton*). [81]

1761 In May, John Wesley stayed for one night in Moffat on his way from Wigton in Cumbria to Edinburgh.

"Before noon we came to Solway-frith. The guide told us, it was not passable. But I resolved to try, and got over well. Having lost ourselves, but twice or thrice, in one of the most difficult roads I ever saw, we came to Moffat in the evening.

Tuesday 28th , we rode partly over the mountains, partly with mountains on either hand, between which was a clear, winding river, and about four in the afternoon reached Edinburgh." [82]

1763 An account of Moffat described it as follows:

"At Moffat, a village in a district of Scotland called Annandale, about thirty-six miles south-west of Edinburgh, are Moffat wells, the most famous mineral waters in Scotland. .... The waters are diuretic, emetic and cathartic, powerfully removing all obstructions of the bowels, and therefore very good against the cholic and nephritic disorders. They are also of service to remove pains in the joints; they are said to be sovereign remedy in scorbutic cases, and the king's evil; and are used both by drinking and bathing. They are supposed to owe their virtue to a sulphureous principle." [83]

1764 In November, John Aiken travelled from Carlisle to Moffat and he was more impressed by Moffat than by what he saw along the way:

"After travelling *(from Carlisle)* some dreary miles in dreadful roads along the flat country, we came to a more hilly one which, though as barren, was more agreeable. At night we arrived at Moffat, which is a good village, adorned with some handsome houses, but sure nothing could exhibit a more complete picture of wretchedness than the few cottages we met on the road, built of mud, and having a kind of breach in the wall for the entrance, and a hole at the top to let out the smoke and let in the light." [84]

1766 James Boswell was back in Moffat. By this time, Boswell was suffering from malaria (contracted in Corsica) and recurrent bouts of urethritis (caused by gonorrhoea) but perhaps his most painful complaint was a chronic case of ingrowing toenails which were operated upon, without anaesthetic, on repeated occasions through his life. Boswell was a chronic alcoholic and he was also addicted to gambling and to prostitutes. In May 1766 came to Moffat, partly to escape an infatuation (".. my fancy is quite inflamed.. ") with his gardener's daughter who was a chambermaid at Auchinleck House, Boswell's property near Ayr. While in Moffat, he struck up a relationship with a Mrs. Dodds, called "Circe" or "the Moffat woman" by Boswell. She became his mistress for the next eighteen months and was the mother of Sally, Boswell's first daughter. From Moffat Boswell wrote a letter to his friend the Rev. William Johnson Temple:

"... I have found in Moffat a lady just in the situation of the one whom you formerly dallied with in Northumberland. I am quite devoted to her.... Love reconciles me to the Scots accent, which from the mouth of a pretty woman is simply and sweetly melodious. It is indeed, and I could engage to make Temple himself swear so in a few months.

I came to Moffat to wash off a few scurvy spots which the warmer climates of Europe had brought out on my skin. I drink the waters, and bathe regularly, and take a great deal of exercise, and have a fine flow of spirits. I am as happy as an unmarried man can be." [85]

1769 Thomas Pennant visited Moffat, where he met the hugely talented John Walker who was then the minister at Moffat:

" ... a small neat town, famous for its spaws *(spas)*; one said to be useful in scrophulous cases, the other a chalybeate, which makes this place much resorted to in summer. Doctor Walker, minister of the place, showed me in manuscript his natural history of the Western Isles, which will do him much credit whenever he favours the world with it." [86]

1769 In August, Bishop Robert Forbes and Mrs. Forbes set off from Edinburgh to Moffat to meet with Bishop Robert Gordon and Laurence and Margaret Oliphant of Gask ("Mr. and Mrs. Lyon"). This was to be a clandestine meeting between Jacobites at which they discussed plans for the continuance of the Stuart line through the marriage of Charles Edward to a Protestant. [20]

The first leg of the journey, from Edinburgh to the Crook Inn, took 9 hours 50 minutes (the Bishop kept very precise records). After a night at the Crook it took them another 3 hours 20 minutes to reach Moffat. Therefore the total journey time from Edinburgh to Moffat was 12 hours 10 minutes:

"The other side of Errick-stane Brae towards Moffat was once a very steep road, insomuch that travellers walked, and machines went empty down and up it; but now of late it is made such a very fine pathed way in the spiral form that coaches and chaises can move easily upon it full of company. When on the top of Errickstane Brae a fine valley of a corn country towards Moffat opens to you, which exhibits a chearing prospect of a beautiful variety.

We arrived at Moffat ¼ before 11 o'clock, and Bishop Gordon with Mr. and Mrs. Lyon came to us about 5 o'clock when we were beginning to tea. At supper I proposed that for a jaunt of pleasure we should go next day to view the Gray Mare's Tail, perhaps the finest fall of water in all Scotland, and about seven long Scots miles from Moffat, which was agreed to.

After driving about two miles, we enter into one of the finest and richest vallies I have ever seen, called the Glen of Moffat Water, standing thick with corn and hay, interspersed with meadow grounds, and bounded on each hand with a

46

ridge of green mountains, decorated with bushes of wood, and with large flocks of sheep feeding and frisking up and down under the eyes of the careful shepherds tending them by day and by night with their sagacious dogs. In this fertile valley there were likewise herds of horses and black cattle, fat and sleek as otters, which upon the sight and rattling of the chaises took fright, stared, snorted, and galloped up and down with ears erect and tails standing out. There was one colt, of a brownish colour beautiful and well shap'd, which Bishop Gordon admired greatly.

When we got into the chaises *(after seeing the Grey Mare's Tail)* Mr. Gordon said; "We cross'd Moffat Water so often that we will now, in our return, count the number," which turned out to be no less than 16, without counting several other crossings of rivulets that discharge themselves from the hills into Moffat Water. But we brought the crossing of the Tail burn into the reckoning. At supper we recounted the beauties and adventures of the chequered scene with great good humour and pleasantry." [87]

1770 John Buncle provided a most informative and graphic account of the Moffat waters. This description is particularly interesting because it provides an estimate of the volume of water produced by the lower well. The daily yield was about 1,280 to 1,360 gallons (5,820 to 6,180 litres), roughly equivalent to the capacity of 27 modern domestic baths:

"There are two medicinal springs or wells, which are separated from one another by a small rock: the higher well lies with its mouth south-east. 'Tis of an irregular square figure, and is about a foot and a half deep. The lower well is surrounded with naked rocks: it forms a small arch of a circle. Its depth is four feet and a half and, by a moderate computation, the two springs yield 40 loads of water in 24 hours, each load containing 64 or 68 Scotch pints; a Scotch pint is two English quarts. The higher shallow well is used for bathing, as it is not capable of being kept so clean as the lower well, on account of the shallowness and the looseness of its parts.

Great is the medicinal virtue of these waters in relieving, inwardly, colics, pains in the stomach, griping of the guts, bilious and nephritic colics; nervous and hysteric colics ; the gravel, by carrying off the quantities of sand, (but does not dissolve the slimy gravel) clearing the urinary passages in a wonderful manner; in curing ischuries *(urine retention)*, and ulcerated kidneys; the gout, the palsy, obstructions of the menses, old gleets *(urethral discharges)*, and barrenness: it is a sovereign remedy in rheumatic and scorbutic pains, even when the limbs are monstrously swelled, useless, and covered with scales. Outwardly, ulcers, tumours, itch, St. Anthony's fire *(ergotism)*, and king's evil *(scrofula)* .

The waters are used by bathing and drinking: to drink in the morning three chopins, six pints or a Scotch quart, four English quarts, at most between the hours of six and eleven. After dinner to drink gradually." [88]

1773 Thomas Bonar toured throughout Britain while he was on holiday from Russia where he was a friend of Dr. Rogerson, who later lived at Dumcrieff. On his way from Glasgow to Bristol, Thomas stopped off at Fourmerkland in Johnstone parish where he stayed with relatives of Dr. Rogerson. Thomas must have had a rough journey, because in a letter to Rogerson he says:

> "I have not travelled over such bad roads during my whole course as from Glasgow to Moffat to see your friends. I shall look upon that as a debt upon you to go 50 miles whenever I desire you to see any friends of mine." [89]

1775 In the winter of this year Mr. McCulloch of Ardwell, a customs commissioner who was noted for his ready wit, left Moffat by coach on his journey to Leith. At about the same time another coach, carrying Samuel Foote the actor, followed the same route. The heavy snow on Ericstane Brae forced both coaches to return to the King's Arms. Such was the severity of the winter that both travellers were to be stuck in Moffat for the next twenty days. McCulloch and Foote were clearly bored and the latter struck upon the following piece of amusement:

"Foote remained quiet for a few hours after breakfast, until he had beat about for game, as he termed it, and he first fixed upon worthy Mrs. Little, his hostess. By some occult means he had managed to get hold of some of the old lady's habiliments, particularly a favourite nightcap. After attiring himself *á la* Mrs. Little, he went into the kitchen and through the house, mimicking the garrulous landlady so very exactly in giving orders, scolding etc. that no servant doubted as to its being the mistress *in propria persona*. This kind of amusement went on for several days for the benefit of the people of Moffat." [90]

1776 Andrew Wight popped into Moffat as part of his tour of Scotland to establish the state of husbandry in the country and he was not the only observer to comment on the undesirable local habit of smearing sheep with tar:

"I arrived at Moffat, which is well known by its medicinal water. The village is remarkably neat and clean. It stands on a sloping gravel, which, with a fine current of air, makes it a wholesome place. It belongs to the estate of Annandale; to the improvement of which the Earl of Hopeton gives great attention, particularly to the breed of sheep, grudging no expense for procuring good rams to cross the breed.

In this high country, unfit for corn, sheep are the only product of the land; and Moffat therefore is a most convenient place for the woollen manufacture. Some time ago the commerce of wool in this country was in a very low state. Much of it was purchased for various manufactures in England in its rudest state, as it was shorn. It was dressed there; and commonly not more than two thirds of the gross weight was made use of; the other third was waste, on account of the tar that is laid on in smearing. This dressed wool was made into coarse stuffs; and any of it that was white enough they manufactured into Kendal cottons. These manufactures were carried by land to Glasgow, through the town of Moffat, and exported to the southern parts of the British colonies of America. What a saving would there be, if these goods were manufactured at Moffat?

Markets, Fairs, Sales and Shows

In April 1662, a charter by Charles II conferred on Moffat the status of a burgh of barony and regality. This charter gave the rights to put up a market cross, and to hold a weekly market and four annual fairs. Friday was to be the weekly market-day and the fairs were to fall on the 18th June, 18th July, 2nd September, and 9th October.

The original market place was opposite the Old Kirkyard gate and the position of the market was marked by small paved circles with a cross line of stones. Some of these can still be seen. The market was moved further up the street in about 1772 to a position opposite the Town Clock.

In 1873, Friday was still the market-day and the other markets were:

Hiring Fair	March (for the hiring of farm servants and workers)
Wool Fair	Fourth Friday of July
Lamb Fair	End of July or beginning of August
Beattock Ram Sale	Biennially in September, day before Moffat Tup Fair
Tup Fair and Show	September, on the Friday after the Falkirk Tryst Hiring
Fair	October
Flower Show	A separate annual event from about 1840 to 1871.
Agricultural Show	Held in September in the 1870s. Joined with the Flower Show in 1872.

In the late 18th Century, fairs and cattle shows were held in a field between the Gallow Hill, the Whins, and the Forester's Cottage. However, it seems that everyone moaned about this site and it was later moved to the Ladyknowe. In 1872 the show was moved to one of the Vicarlands holms.

During the period 1850 – 1880, the Beattock Ram Sale was attended by throngs of buyers from all over the United Kingdom. In 1851, for example, almost 2,000 persons travelled to a field opposite the Beattock Inn and every item of stock was sold. Wool prices reached their height in 1865, partly due to the American Civil War and the consequent cotton shortages. The pre-eminent breeder in southern Scotland at this time was Mr. Brydon from Moodlaw (adjacent to the Samye Ling Tibetan Centre at Eskdalemuir) and Kinnelhead.

The Moffat Tup Market reached its height during the same period when up to 1,500 tups would be sold in a single day to buyers from all over Scotland. The most successful breeders in the Moffat area at this time included Welsh of Ericstane, Johnstone of Archbank, Johnstone of Caplegill, Johnstone of Hunterheck, and Anderson of Reddings.

The Hiring Markets were occasions of high anxiety for the people of Moffat because of the well-founded fear of widespread drunkenness and unruly behaviour (see entry for the year **1861**).

I surveyed the lands of Dumcrief with peculiar pleasure, because every corner bore the marks of genius. (Mr. Clerk) has clearly demonstrated that the great proportion of tar used in smearing sheep is hurtful both to the animal and to the wool ...... In one word, by these means, Mr. Clerk was able to advance the value of his wool from 5s. per stone to 13s.

The Earl of Hopeton sent a ram of Mr. Cully's breed to Gillespie (farmer in Caplegill and Carrifran) in September 1773. His progeny bore better wool than that of his other sheep, and in greater quantity. But they proved too delicate for their pasture; and their wool became yearly coarser, and in less quantity. In November 1774, Lord Hopeton sent Gillespie a ram of Bakewell's kind, but with as little success. Mr. Gillespie thinks that he is too short-legged for scrambling through rocks and mountains, and for scraping the snow from the grass." [91]

1778 David Loch made a tour throughout Scotland and reported on the state of trade and manufacturing. His report on Moffat included the following:

"Thomas, John, and Adam Reid at Moffat give an account of a particular kind of goods, made at this place, called stuffs, which are sold on the English side, and the demand is so great that it cannot be answered. They also manufacture plaids or mauds, and blankets to a great extent, of which article they made 3,000 yards last year. There is another article they manufacture, called checked serge. It is made into hunting coats, a light garb for summer wear, and answers very well for children's cloathes. They also make lastings, mancoes, flannels, and serges, which are mostly exported into Holland. Here are about 50 looms all in the woollen branches. Serges, shalloons, duffles, blankets, coarse cloths of all denominations.

The ordinary quantity of wool manufactured in and about Moffat annually is about 1,250 stones. Mr. Ewart has a fine breed of sheep of Bakewell and Culley's kind; but there is one custom very prejudicial to the woollen manufacture.

Which is, the practice of laying on a long tar mark on their sheep, mostly about half a yard long that renders all the wool useless where the tar mark is laid, and which adds considerably to the weight of the wool. It is the opinion of Messrs. Reid and many others, that the more grease and the less tar that is employed, it will be better for the wool, and likewise be more beneficial to the sheep; that the tar mark ought to be totally abolished, and that a boust *(ointment)* ought to be used for marking the sheep." [92]

1780   Elizabeth Sarah Villa-Real Gooch visited Moffat and she seems to have thought little of Moffat's funereal customs:

"We reached Moffat on the fourth day, and were then told that it was impossible to pursue our journey; every carriage that had attempted it for the last week being returned. We walked about the town, saw the spa, and a diversion they call "curling" which consists in several men throwing stones over the ice with iron handles to them, and from forty to fifty pounds weight. We observed also three large stones erected near the town, which they told us were to the memory of three generals who had been killed there, but we could find no trace of inscription on them. We saw a funeral, where numbers assisted, but which had no other ceremony than putting the corpse into the ground without form of prayer, and the friends regaling on their return at the house of the deceased with victuals, wines etc." [93]

1781   In October, the Rev. William Turner made the journey from Leeds to Glasgow, taking two days and nights to complete the trip:

"We entered Scotland at the famous Gretna Green, and proceeded through a dreary country, by Locherby, Moffat and Hamilton, to Glasgow. At these three places we found very tolerable inns, especially at Moffat; but at two little paltry places where we stopped besides, the worst places I can conceive." [94]

1782   James Edward Smith visited Moffat and, like Thomas Pennant in 1769, he met the minister and naturalist Dr. John Walker, known locally as the "mad minister of Moffat". James later wrote to his father from Edinburgh:

"I left Carlisle on Tuesday night at eight o'clock, and arrived at Moffat next morning by five. This is a neat pleasant town, where there is a sulphureous spring much resorted to: the town is at present full of genteel company, and they have dancing almost every night. Here I found Dr. Walker, as I expected: he has a good house and noble garden here, which he will leave in November, as he will then remove to a place three miles only from Edinburgh, where he has got a living in exchange for Moffat. I spent that day and the next very happily with the Doctor: he is a very agreeable man, the life and soul of Moffat. His loss will be equally felt by the gay, the industrious, and the unhappy." *(Walker was about to move to a new ministry at Colinton in Edinburgh.)* [95]

1783 Lady Glenorchy and Lady Henrietta Hope (afterwards Lady Melville) visited Moffat. In August, Lady Glenorchy wrote from Moffat that:

"The Lord has been pleased to visit me by sickness once more, after having attained to a measure of health I had not known for several years past. He gave me health for a season, and now he has taken it away ; blessed be his name, for he doth all things well. This *(Moffat)* is a sad benighted place, but there is a remnant in it that fear God." [96]

One of Lady Glenorchy's biographers had a turn of phrase which, although peculiar to us now, would not have raised any eyebrows at that time.

"In June, her faithful friend *(Lady Henrietta)* went to Moffat, for the purpose of drinking goat's whey, as she was in a delicate state of health, and her ladyship *(Lady Glenorchy)* soon followed her. While there, she received much benefit from intercourse with a few pious persons in humble life. One of these poor Christian plebeians, unpolished by learning, but earnest in prayer, and depending upon grace, had lain nine years in her bed, rejoicing in the goodness of God." [97]

Another biographer of Lady Glenorchy said much the same thing but in different way:

"She was only 41 years of age, and a little improvement occurring in her condition, she cheerfully went to the Scotch watering-place, Moffat, possibly to adopt what had been her friends' practice for years, that of drinking goats' whey. Lady Henrietta Hope was already at Moffat when Lady Glenorchy joined them there. Indefatigable in good works when she had any approach to strength, she visited personally and sought to instruct and comfort the sick poor about Moffat." [98]

1784 James Currie came to Moffat in June, July, and early August when he was close to dying from consumption (he finally succumbed to this disease in 1805). His relatives had persuaded him to seek his own cure at Moffat Well and he took new strength from the deep-rooted peace and stillness of the hills and valleys. After only a few days of this treatment he was able to renounce his rigorous abstention from wine, beer and meat. He met with Edinburgh friends along the High Street, at the Black Bull, and at the old bowling green. From the day he left Moffat for Liverpool he carried an association of the lands of Dumcrieff with perfect peace. [99]

1785 William Thomson gained a mixed impression of the locality:

"Between Dumfries and Moffat .... there is not a house in which you can find any accommodation that is tolerable. Dine at Moffat, a very small town, with some tolerable houses in it, which are let to invalids who come to this place for the benefits of the water. The land in these parts might be made more profitable, both to the landlord and tenant, by enclosing the lower parts of the hills, and screening them from the rudeness of the climate by trees. For in this barren tract there is scarcely a tree or wood of any kind to be seen, except a plantation of firs to the north of the town *(probably the Gallow Hill)*, which are yet in their infancy, but which clearly prove that trees will grow, if the inhabitants will only take the trouble to plant them. There is a good house here, belonging to Lord Hopetoun; and the next best is the inn, where there is good accommodation, and an ordinary, as at Matlock and Buxton." [100]

1786 John Knox (not *the* John Knox) passed through Moffat on his way to a tour of the Highlands and Hebrides:

> "The country around Dumfries is in high cultivation, but these appearances soon vanish, as we advance towards Moffat. It has been affirmed, that while these southern countries remain under strict entails, while they are no longer frequented by the proprietors, but left solely to the management of factors or stewards, all the feeble efforts of a poor commonalty will be inadequate to the great object of internal improvement, in a country where lime is scarce, and where coals are burdened with a high duty, besides a water and a land carriage, proportioned to the distance of each district from the Solway Firth.
>
> Moffat, a small town, lies twenty-one miles from Dumfries, and has long been noted for its spas; on which account it is much frequented in the summer season. The country northwards becomes almost entirely pastoral. The ascent of the road from Moffat towards the summit of these mountains, presents a most extensive view to the south, where the prospect is bounded by the mountains of Cumberland, whose appearance, tho' at a great distance, is majestic and sublime; and here an English traveller takes a parting view of his native country. " [101]

1787 John Brown (later to become the Rev. John Brown) had a bad early experience at Moffat Well but on this occasion the waters were not to blame:

> "I was bitten severely by a little dog when with my mother at Moffat Wells, being then three years of age, and I have remained 'bitten' ever since in the matter of dogs. I remember that little dog, and can at this moment not only recall my pain and terror - I have no doubt I was to blame - but also her face: and were I allowed to search among the shades in the cynic Elysian fields, I could pick her out still." [102]

1787 A correspondent calling himself "Etonensis" insisted that there were only three Scottish spas of real significance: Peterhead, Pannanich (at Ballater) and Moffat. For Etonensis, the favoured spa was Moffat:

"The resort to these places has, of late years, been frequent, and that too by persons of bon ton (the fashionable elite)." [103]

1788 This was an auspicious year for Moffat and the circumstances were colourfully described by John Oswald Mitchell:

"On the morning of Monday 7th July 1788, Moffat was early astir. At 4.00 a.m. it was high change at the King's Arms, the landlord out on the steps, the landlady behind him, the servant lass behind her, hostlers and postboys hanging about, and four horses in new ands shining harness whisking their tales in front of the inn; at every door in the High Street some one stood, heads appeared and reappeared at every window.

The mail, the London and Glasgow mail – none of your ramshackle pair horse diligences, but one of John Palmer's new mail coaches, spick and span, with four spanking horses – was due on its first run.; it was high time – Edinburgh had been having her mail ever since 10th April – and presently, heralded by the fire of its pistols and the toot-toot of its horn, out from the Wamphray road by Holm Street, with scarlet-coated coachman and guard, the mail drove in, pulled up at the King's Arms and after some refreshments, some drinking of healths, and shaking of hands, drove on with fresh horses for Elvanfoot.

And from that Monday, 7th July 1788, till Tuesday 15th February 1848, when it was blocked by the Caledonian Railway, the London, Carlisle, and Glasgow mail, though not always through Moffat, drove north and drove south, Sunday and Saturday, summer and winter, fair weather and foul. ." [104]

1788 A French traveller passed through the area. In reading this account one should remember that this was the eve of the French Revolution and that the writer was an adherent to its principles, including the abolition of feudalism and a unfair systems of taxation:

"The countryside around Dumfries is well cultivated but this beautiful appearance disappears as one approaches Moffat. It is certain that this southernmost part of Scotland will always be poorly cultivated as long as taxes are as high as they are today, and as long as the owners living far from their fields will leave them to the care of mercenary hands. The manures and fertilisers which are required to improve the land are very expensive and the cost of transport is high.

Moffat .... has been renowned for a long time for its mineral waters. These attract many visitors who are so ill, their lives so sad, that they seek a place where a cure may be bought in this place where wild nature does not give any respite. To the north of Moffat the countryside is almost entirely inhabited by couples which carry out a life as rural as their herds." [105]

1789 At some time between 13th August and 25th September, Robert Burns met in Moffat with William Nicol, the notoriously brutal headmaster of Edinburgh High School, and Allan Masterton. The location of this meeting may have been a small inn, owned by Archibald Blacklock, next to the old entrance to the Kirkyard. [106] They all had such a good time that Burns penned "Willie Brew'd A Peck O' Maut". Burns' note to the song was as follows:

'This air is *(Allan)* Masterton's; the song mine. The occasion of it was this: Mr William Nicol, of the High School, Edinburgh, during the autumn vacation being at Moffat, honest Allan—who was at that time on a visit to Dalswinton—and I went to pay Nicol a visit. We had such a joyous meeting, that Mr Masterton and I agreed, each in our own way, that we should celebrate the business." [107]

1790 On 31st May, John Wesley paid another visit to Moffat following his earlier visit in 1761. Wesley was now 86 years of age. This extract tells us little about Moffat but a good deal about Wesley's zeal and the times taken to travel in those days:

"We set out at two *(in the morning, from Glasgow)* and came to Moffat soon after three in the afternoon: taking fresh horses, we reached Dumfries between six and seven, and found the congregation waiting." [108]

1791 Robert Heron provided a factual description of the town:

"The town of Moffat has a manufacture of coarse woollen stuffs, but it is chiefly supported by its mineral springs which attract much genteel company. This town contains many good houses, built for the accommodation of those who visit this place for the sake of the waters. The mountain of Hartfell is about three thousand feet high. There is a beautiful plain on its top, of sufficient extent for a horse-race, and commanding a most extensive prospect. ..... The country is barren of wood except in the neighbourhood of the town; and the ground is generally employed in feeding sheep and black cattle. In the moss called Drumcrief, large oak and birch trees are frequently dug up quite fresh and entire though they must, without doubt, have lain there for many centuries." [109]

1791 It was in about this year that Messrs. Busby, two coal-viewers from Northumberland, were retained by a consortium of Dumfriesshire gentlemen to carry out a survey of mineral resources. They carried out some coal trials and some remains of shallow shafts with rims of upcast spoil are still visible on the south bank of the Coalpit Burn, about 1,000 metres to the west of Rivox. [110] [111]

The Busbys recommended a locality in the Frenchland Burn as a likely source of slate and they also bored for marl (a source of fertiliser for lime-deficient soils) at Lochhouse. Dr. Singer, in his later book on the state of agriculture in Dumfriesshire, recommended trial boring for coal at Nethermiln but this ceased at an early date. [112]

1792 In May Dr. James Currie, who had recently bought Dumcrieff, wrote from Liverpool to some friends to describe his initial impressions. It is worth recording his letter at some length, both for his enthusiasm and for the wealth of detailed observation. He was clearly besotted by the beauty of the place although his description of some of the local inhabitants was a little insensitive:

"You cannot think how beautiful the house and valley of Dumcrief looked from the bridge as I passed: sheltered by the woods and mountains, it seemed to enjoy a perfect calm. I saw a great crowd of people in the court, so I did not drive up as I intended; and I was glad of this afterwards, for I found they were selling the goods of the inhabitants (a brother's family of the late proprietor) by public auction. Hearing this, I kept away that afternoon.

I met at Moffat some friends from Edinburgh and Dumfries, who were waiting for me; and in about an hour after we arrived, my sister from Edinburgh, who, hearing I was to be there on that day, had set off to meet me. We took lodgings next morning, and kept house together the five following days. On Wednesday I was up by break of day, and you can form no notion of my alacrity. What though the morning was lowering, and the wind blew from the east? What cared I for the wind? It shouted in my ears without being heeded.

I mounted a horse that had been provided for me, and in half an hour was on the top of Hunterheck hill. This is an eminence (in Lancashire it would be a mountain) that rises on the northernmost point of the estate of Dumcrief, and from which I could see the whole as distinctly as if every part was at my feet. I found that this property of mine was a peninsula, bounded by two beautiful rivers (Moffat and Annan) on each side, and terminated by their junction to the south. The banks of these rivers, especially the former, I found well wooded; and several eminences besides, enclosed and covered with trees. The mountain on which I stood was perfectly verdant and covered with sheep; forming a striking contrast with the huge, black and frowning Alps that rose around it across the valleys, and hid their heads in the clouds. About two miles to the south, almost concealed from the view by surrounding wood, I saw the house of Dumcrief; and having surveyed it with striking emotions of pleasure, without approaching it, I returned to Moffat to breakfast.

You cannot think how I felt my sensations lightened by this mountain air. I was braced in body and mind, and felt that care and sorrow passed me on either side. After breakfast I went out again, a friend with me, and a farmer who served as a guide. We now approached the house, but not directly, for the people being a sort of savages, I did not wish to come on them at once. I took a turn or two in the wood within their sight, to show them that I was a Christian, and sent a message, hoping it would not be inconvenient to them if I should call.

The house is an old house, with walls cannon proof: there is one modern room, a very fine one; another tolerable, and nine bed-rooms. I speak from what I saw afterwards, when I had convinced these people that I was a harmless sort of man. Before the door, there is a lawn about the size of a large bowling-green, and used as such in Sir George Clerk's *(Sir George Clerk-Maxwell's [113])* time, surrounded by trees of perhaps 200 years old. On one of these hangs a bell to ring the family to dinner, and perhaps to prayers, on which I saw "1612", with a cross above it, marking a Catholic origin. I cannot describe the beauties about the house, out of the windows of which you see the river Moffat winding along at your feet, and may plunge, if you please, into this transparent stream. The opposite banks are finely wooded, and a Chinese bridge is thrown across. Above the house is a mill for grinding corn, which some would call a defect, but which I call a beauty; and above that, the garden, in certainly the most singularly romantic situation that can well be conceived. On the one side it is bounded by the river, which is here banked in, but without any wall; and on the other, by the side of a hill, covered with impenetrable wood. The river here making a sudden bend, you are entirely shut out from the house, &c., below ; the woods exclude you to the south and west; but to the east and north-east there is a view surpassing in beauty and sublimity, consisting of the windings of this stream, of the plains beyond it, of the gradually ascending hills, at first green and covered with sheep, and towering upwards to the top of Hartfell, about ten miles distant, and rising perpendicularly above 3,000 feet.

The garden itself is laid out in a very fine taste; and when you examine its boundary towards the wood, you find it made by another river, which glides through the trees, and which is no other than the stream which drives the mill below, taken off from the Moffat above the garden. I could not but admire the genius, as well as taste, shown in converting this deformity, as some would call it, into a beauty of the first order; and while I examined it, I could not but apostrophise the spirit of Sir George Clerk, the former owner of this property, and the planner of its improvements, who died about eight years ago, and who, if departed ghosts are ever suffered to review this world, may perhaps sometimes wander among the groves he loved." [114]

Dr. Currie wrote in the same year from Liverpool to his near-relation, another Dr. James Currie, who resided in Richmond, Virginia:

"I know not whether I mentioned to you a purchase I made of land in Annandale, about the beginning of the year. It was the estate of Dumcrief, close by Moffat, which once belonged to Mr. Clerk, afterwards Sir George Clerk, the laird of Middlebie. In the beginning of May I went down to that country for a few days to look at my estate. I was greatly pleased with it; a more beautiful spot I hardly ever saw. I indulge the hope that I may one day reside there, and spend my latter days in tranquillity and peace. I know how generally fallacious such expectations are; but, for all that, they gild the present moments of toil, anxiety, and care." [62]

Janet Little (1759 - 1813) came from Ecclefechan. She had only "a common education" but she loved reading and by 1788 had acquired some reputation as a "rustic poetess", when she became a chambermaid or nurse with Mrs. Frances Dunlop of Dunlop House, Ayrshire, the friend and correspondent of Robert Burns. In 1789 she was put in charge of the dairy at Loudon Castle. One source describes Janet as "a very tall masculine woman, with dark hair, and features somewhat course." Mrs. Dunlop, in a letter to Burns said: "Her outside promises nothing; her mind only bursts forth on paper."

We have no idea if Janet visited Moffat but we do know that this poem was published in 1792. Among the subscribers to her collection of poems were Burns, Mrs Dunlop, and James Boswell, to whom she had hoped to dedicate the book. Boswell had advised her to dedicate it instead to a titled lady, who turned out to be the 11-year-old Flora, Countess of Loudoun. [115]

To Nell at Moffat Well
by Janet Little

On the delightful banks of Mein,
The muse laments in pensive strain;
The nymphs assembl'd on the green,
Of Nelly's absence all complain.

Our rural swains no joys can find,
But still in pensive silence mourn;
With heads upon the turf reclin'd
They sigh, and wish your swift return.

Oft have they curs'd fair Moffat town,
With all the virtues of the Well;
The sprightly Beau, and rustic clown,
Of Nelly's charms delight to tell.

Dear maid, it is for you alone,
They spend whole days and nights in sighs
And will you disregard their moan,
And all their plaintive notes despise?

'Tis Autumn now, the fertile field,
Rich Ceres decks with yellow grain;
With joy we would our sickles wield,
If Nelly deign'd to grace the plain.

Come now and of our labours share;
None better can that weapon ply;
O mitigate Philander's care,
Whose toil seems less when you are nigh.

Once more, dear Nell, I'd wish to see
You cheerful join the rural throng;
Your presence would enhance our glee,
And sweetly animate my song.

1792 In August, John Lettice passed through Moffat on his journey across Great Britain. He provides a perceptive and amusing description of the town:

"After we left Lockerbie we found ourselves on an excellent road .... which ran on the declivity of some lofty wild hills ... the scenery brought us to some extensive plantations surrounding a handsome mansion (Dumcrieff) at present in the possession of Dr. Curry of Liverpool. Passing the river which flows by Dr. Curry's grounds, we reached the town, consisting of houses not ill-built, but all turned with their gable ends to a large pleasant area: the market place. Cottages of meaner construction running in a line with these superior edifices, and forming streets behind them, make up the town; a place of some bustle on various accounts.

The poorer people are employed in manufacturing coarse woollen stuffs, chiefly plaids of small chequer work ... of more elegant and less glaring patterns than those made in the Highlands. The better order of inhabitants are partly supported by disposing of the produce of the loom, and partly by letting accommodations to invalids; the rheumatic, the scrophulous, the hypochondriac, or the idle; the last most numerous of the three. Indeed without this useful tribe, with whom all waters agree, though their case is helpless, few of these places would prosper ..... Whether alkalis, or acids, constitute their predominant qualities is of little consequence to those who resort to these amusing spaws, with much less hope of curing themselves, than of killing time.

But the principal movement of the town of Moffat, during our short stay in it, arose, as we understood, it generally does, from the continual passage of travellers to and from Glasgow, Edinburgh, Dumfries etc. who keep a large inn very much alive day and night. The many successive arrivals and departures of various rank and figure, in carriages, on horseback, or on foot, the constant scene before our window, helped considerably to cheer a very dark and rainy day. We had frequent occasion to admire the hardiness of idle spectators, and of persons stopping each other in the market place, to converse during the heaviest showers of rain. Women too, and some not of the lowest class, without hat or bonnet, we saw in conversation *tête-à-tête*, discoursing with as much earnestness, as if perfectly insensible of the weather .... Though no people love better to be warm and snug in their houses and cottages, than the North Britons, no other in Europe perhaps will be found, who meet the severest cold with more patience and resolution." [116]

1793 Colonel Alexander Ross arrived but, alas, he lived only long enough to record his aspirations for, and not his impressions of, Moffat. This case emphasises the need for early intervention. A stone in the Old Kirkyard bears the following inscription:

"Here is interred the body of Colonel Alex. Ross of Calrossie, Ross-shire, who died in Moffat, June 1793. He came there in hopes, from the use of the water, to obtain remission of long and painful illness but, unhappily for his friends, he had too long delayed resorting to them and was cut off by his complaint before he had opportunity of trying their efficacy." [117]

1794 The artist James Skene visited Loch Skene with his friend (Sir) Walter Scott. James's description of the journey will be familiar to those who have made the walk:

"One of our earliest expeditions was to visit the wild scenery of the mountainous tract above Moffat, including the cascade of the Grey Mare's Tail and the dark tarn called Loch Skene. In our ascent to the lake we got completely bewildered in the thick fog which generally envelopes the rugged features of that lonely region; and, as we were groping through the maze of bogs, the ground gave way, and down went horse and horsemen pell-mell into the slough of peaty mud and black water, out of which, entangled as we were with our plaids and floundering nags, it was no easy matter to get extricated .... As it was, we rose like the spirits of the bog, covered *cap-a-pie* with slime, to free themselves from which our wily ponies took to rolling about on the heather, and we had nothing for it but following their example.

At length as we approached the gloomy loch, a huge eagle heaved himself from the margin, and rose right over us, screaming his scorn of the intruders; and altogether it would be impossible to picture any thing more desolately savage than the scene which opened ... Much of the scenery of *Old Mortality* was drawn from that day's ride." [118]

1794   John Naismyth visited Moffat on his tour of Southern Scotland to report on the state of sheep farming in the region:

"The woollen manufacture is begun in this neighbourhood, where there is good conveniency of water to drive machinery. Two brothers of the name of Dickson have a most complete working house. Messrs. Irwin and Craig have lately erected a manufacture for teasing, scribbling, carding, and spinning wool. Housewives in the neighbourhood get their wool prepared here at 3s.6d. per stone, and the prepared wool is carried away, to be spun at home.

Short sheep *(sheep with shorter fleece than long sheep)* are generally kept around Moffat. It *(the wool)* goes mostly to the north of England, and dealers come here and buy it. The farmers are now under the necessity to begin to wash their sheep before shearing, in order to please the wool merchants, who refuse to buy unwashed wool.

Lambs are weaned about 15th July, and put for a few days on good pasture which had been saved for them. They are afterwards led to high benty land, where they remain till they are brought to the hog fence for the winter, which is the best sheltered and most grassy part of the farm. Wedders are sold either in lambs or hogs. The rams are admitted to the ewes on Martinmas day *(11ᵗʰ November)* and to the gimmers 14 days after." [119]

1794 In December, James Boswell visited Moffat where his daughters had been staying. He collected them on his journey from Edinburgh to London and took them back to Moffat in January 1795. [120]

Announcement in the *Dumfries Weekly Journal* 1794 [121]

1795 The Rev. William MacRitchie of Clunie in Perthshire kept a diary of his tour through Great Britain. Having stayed overnight at Bield in Tweedsmuir he rode down Ericstane Brae to Moffat:

"Arrive at Rae's Inn to breakfast at eleven o'clock a.m. .... Go out to the Well and drink of the water: strong sulphur; it smells of rotten eggs, very forbidding; its taste not quite so disagreeable. It is thought good for scorbutic complaints. The Hartfell Spaw for consumptive ones. Set out for Dumfries, and pass by Raehills, a new seat of the Earl of Hopeton." [122] [123]

1795 It took Robert Owen two days and three nights of incessant travelling to get from Manchester to Glasgow and he mentions that the coach had to cross a well-known dangerous mountain at midnight, called Erickstane Brae, which was then always passed with fear and trembling. [124]

1795 The Reverend J. H. Michell travelled throughout England and Scotland with the twenty-year-old 11th Duke of Somerset. Near Moffat, the travellers had an object lesson in "ducal irresponsibility" when they observed the hillsides denuded of trees by William Douglas, the 4th Duke of Queensberry. The Duke had done this to pay a dowry for Maria Fagniani, whom he fancied was his daughter, when she married the Earl of Yarmouth. This action also incurred the immediate wrath of Burns, who loathed the Duke (" Drumlanrig's haughty Grace ... That reptile wears a ducal crown"), and the later wrath of Wordsworth ("Degenerate Douglas! Oh! the unworthy lord"). [125] [126]

1797 Dr. Thomas Garnett, Professor of Natural Philosophy at Glasgow University, visited Moffat with his family. He met with Dr. Johnstone, a medical practitioner in Moffat, who provided Garnett with an account of the medical uses of the waters which he incorporated in his book of 1800.

1798 John Housman kept a journal of his tour through Scotland. He approached Upper Annandale from the north and his impression of the houses up the Annan Water contrasts with his more favourable account of the town itself:

"In this dale the farm-houses and cottages are thatched, and generally very mean. The holm or level land by the sides of the river is narrow, not more in general than 100 to 250 yards broad, from which the cultivated ground rises in irregular waves up to the mountains. The soil is tolerably good, and near Moffat there is a very fertile tract.

Moffat is a small town but for neatness I have not seen many to equal it. It is chiefly composed of one very wide street, with numerous alleys on each side opening into the fields and gardens. Here are several elegant modern houses, which seem to be occupied by people in easy circumstances. The church is likewise a neat edifice, as is the parsonage or *manse* (provincially so called) ..... Moffat contains some good inns being upon the great road from Carlisle to Edinburgh and

Glasgow, and likewise possessing a spa, or mineral water, being much frequented in the season.

Before I left Moffat this morning I observed several people from the country coming early into town and generally with a bottle of milk, and a small bundle of provisions. On inquiry I understood these were pious people on religious business, this being a fast and preaching day among a congregation of dissenters called Burgher Seceders. On this day they do no other work besides attending their devotions." [127]

1799   The Honourable Mrs Sarah Murray of Kensington wrote:

"You must be sure to set out very early from Lanark, that you may reach Moffat before dark, it being impossible to put up at Elvan Foot; you can there only change horses, and those you will seldom get very good, for that country being very hilly, the poor horses are worked to death. Just before you descend the long and steep hill that leads down into Annandale, you will join the Edinburgh road to Moffat, and you will then be not far off the source of Tweed. Moffat is situated near the head of Annandale, and is distant from Elvan Foot, 14 miles.

The country about Moffat is worth looking at, and the inn there is very good .... During the night which I passed at Moffat it had poured with rain ... I crossed a branch of the Annan by Duncrief House (*sic*), finely shaded by wood, and the water dashing furiously close to it. Cornal Tower is on the other side of the water, and is also surrounded by thick wood, at the base of vast mountains." [128]

Beld Craig Linn and Garpol Glen

Many visitors to Moffat in the 19th Century spent a good deal of time walking in the surrounding countryside. More adventurous hikes to the summits of the hills were relatively uncommon and difficult to achieve for those wearing the fashionable clothes of the day. Two of the most popular walks were to Beld Craig and Garpol. For those with less energy or inclination, coaches were available to take the visitor to these attractions.

Beld Craig (also known as Belle Craig or Bell Craig) was described in 1800 by Thomas Garnett and seventy years later this walk from Moffat was described in detail in the guide books and newspapers. Walkers were directed along the Old Carlisle Road to Dumcrieff from where a short detour was recommended by New Mills to Three Waters Foot. Having followed the track which eventually leads to Breconside a footpath took the visitor down the wooded dell to the Deil's Bottom. The path led first to the bald (*beld*) rock which gave the Linn its name and which was described in John McDiarmid's guidebook of 1852 in awesome terms: "The height of the rock we could not exactly ascertain; but the eyeballs are strained in scanning its dimension". The next feature was the Weeping Rock at the foot of which is a deep little hole known as the Devil's footmark ("imprinted by no less an individual than his Infernal Majesty"). The path then led to the head of the Linn and the waterfall running in a fissure of sandstone: a rustic bridge over the burn afforded fine views. Along the way visitors were encouraged to collect ferns and flowering plants and to observe the peregrine falcons which nested on the Craig.

Garpol Glen (also known as Girpell, Gartpool and Garpel) first came to popular notice when, on 15th July 1826, a Moffat shopkeeper called William Walker discovered another source of chalybeate water running down the face of a rock. The main medical use of this water was for gargles. The walk from Moffat led over Coats Hill where visitors were encouraged to stop and admire the view from the rocky outcrop beside what is now the 4th green on the golf course. The route then went over the Caledonian Railway and the Evan and then to the foot of the Glen alongside the railway. A series of neat footpaths and stairs took the visitor to the falls at the head of the Glen, above which a rustic summer house stood facing towards the Gallow Hill, Birnock Cloves, and Hartfell (this summer house was later transported to Station Park and is now the ticket office there). The summer house and the neat paths along the Glen were laid out at the instigation of Isabella Butler-Johnstone, the wife of the owner of Auchen Castle from the 1850s to the 1870s. Auchen Castle was then sold to William Younger in 1879. The walk to Garpol Glen was still popular in the 1890s and visitors had to first obtain a ticket, given free by any of the shopkeepers in Moffat.

Dumfries-shire.   **MOFFAT, &c.**   **Pigot & Co.'s**

*** *The names without address are in* MOFFAT.

GENTRY & CLERGY.
Barrie Mr. Thos. Poldean, Wamphray
Carruthers Samuel, esq. (of Mill) Wamphray
Carruthers William, esq. (of Senerish hill), Wamphray
Culvin Rev. Dr. Robert, Johnstone
Corrie Mr. Hope, Pumplawburn, Wamphray
Dickson Rev. Charles, Wamphray
Hope Capt. Charles, R. N. Larch hill

GENTRY, &c.—Continued.
Rogerson John, esq. M.D. (of Wamphray) Dunerieff [Wamphray
Rogerson John, esq. (of Girthhead)
Singers Rev. Dr. William, Kirkpatrick Juxta
Tod Mr. Raecleuch
Tod Mr. Peter, Meikleholmside
Tod Mrs. Robert, Heathery haugh
Welsh James, esq. (of Earlhaugh) Braefoot [lands
Younger William, esq. of Craiglelands
ACADEMIES & SCHOOLS.
ACADEMY (and boarding establishment for gentlemen)—Alexander Steele, *rector ;* Jno. Gordon, *usher*
INFANTS' SCHOOL, Miss Thomson, *mistress*
Johnston Ebenezer
Mitchell William
BAKERS.
Brown William
Carmichael Mary
Moffat John
Steele William
BANKERS.
GLASGOW UNION BANKING COMPY. (Branch)—(draw on the Parent Establishment, Edinburgh, and on Jones, Loyd and Co. London) —David Jardine, agent
BLACKSMITHS.
Brown William   Little Michael
Dalling George   Porteous John
Halliday George   Thomson Andw.
BOOT & SHOE MAKERS.
Coutts William   Halliday John
Davidson Thos.   Henderson Jas.
Grieve George   Little John
Grieve William   Neilson John
DRESS MAKERS & MILLINRS.
Johnston Agnes Jane
Johnston Janet
Lunham Agnes
M'Night Margaret
Mitchell M.
Wilson Jane
FIRE, &c. OFFICE AGENTS.
ALLIANCE, Alexander Johnston
CALEDONIAN, James M'Millan
INSURANCE COMPANY OF SCOTLAND, William Tait
FLESHERS.
Cartmer John
Halliday William
Johnston Alexander
Rogerson William (& spirit dealer)
GROCERS & SPIRIT DEALERS.
Kerr Jane [butter]
M'Millan James (and stamp distri-
Moffat Francis
Russell John
Stewart William

Jardine Thomas, esq. Craigeburn
Jardine Thomas, esq. of Granton
Johnston Mr. John, Hunterheck
Johnston Mr. Michael, Archbank
Johnston Peter, esq. of Harthope
Johnston Walter, esq. (of Bodesbeck)
Capplegill
Johnstone Rev. Alexander, Manse
Johnstone Major Jno. Langshawbush
Johnstone John James Hope, esq.
M. P. (of Annandale) Raehills

Tait Alleson
Wilson Helen
INNS.
Beatock Inn (posting) Thos. Wilson
Black Bull, Robert Anderson
Spur (posting) Jane Cranstoun
Star, Robert Charters
IRONMONGER.
M'Millan James (& iron merchant)
JOINERS AND CARPENTERS.
Aitchison John and Son
Brown John
Carruthers James
Grieve John
Hamilton & Williamson (and mill-wrights, and millers)
Henderson & Grieve
Sanderson James
Thompson John
LINEN & WOOLLEN DRAPERS.
Anderson James
Burnie Robert
Montgomery Joseph and Co.
Tait William
LODGING HOUSES.
Beattie John   M'Millan Saml.
Bowes Henry (& Mathieson Adam
bourding)   Morrison Alex.
Craig Alexander   Mounile Wm.
Dickson James   Patterson Mrs.
Dickson William   Proudfoot Mrs.
Goldie Marion   Thomas
Grieve Thomas   Rae Mrs. James
Grieve Walter   Russell John
Grieve William   Smith George
Hamilton James   Tait William
Johnston Alex.   Williamson Jas.
Johnston John   Wilson Helen
MASONS & BUILDERS.
Johnston James
Morrison Alexander
MEAL DEALERS.
Bell John (and grain)
Burgess William (and barley)
Carmichael Mary (and barley)
SADDLERS.
Johnston James
Wilson John
STRAW HAT MAKERS.
Johnson Mary
Johnston Elspeth
Lindsay and Craig
Scott Janet
SURGEONS AND DRUGGISTS.
Dalgliesh James
Johnston James
Smith George, R. N. (and dealer in stationery and perfumery)
TAILORS.
Brown John   Cowan John
Carruthers Sa-   Cowan Samuel
muel   Geddes David
Cowan James   Amos

Johnstone Captain William Hope, R. N. Moffat house
Marjoribanks Mrs. Mary,
Moffat Mr. Wm. Craigbeck
Monteath Rev. John, Moffat
Patterson Rev. Henry, Gateside, Wamphray
Proudfoot Mrs. Thomas, of Craigeburn
Rogerson David, esq. (of Leithenhall), Wamphray

Grieve Archibald   Moffat Adam
Hastie John   Riddle William
WATCH & CLOCK MAKERS.
Graham John
Leithead James
Russell Hugh (and jeweller)
Wightman Alexander
Miscellaneous.
Dickson James, woollen manufacturer and dyer
Dinwoodie Peter, vintner
Easton John, clogger
Finis John, plasterer
Grieve Wm. stocking manufacturer
Jardine Matthew, nailer
Kennedy Adam, sheriff's officer
Mathieson Adam, brewer, Amos pl
Robertson Jos. professor of dancing
Sanderson James, cooper
SUBSCRIPTION LIBRARY, James Millan, secretary

PLACES OF WORSHIP.
ESTABLISHED CHURCH, Kirkpatrick Juxta—Rev. Dr. William Singers
ESTABLISHED CHURCH, Moffat—Rev. Alexander Johnstone
ESTABLISHED CHURCH, Gateside, Wamphray—Rev. Henry Patterson
ESTABLISHED CHURCH, Wamphray—Rev. Charles Dickson
UNITED SECESSION CHAPEL, Moffat—Rev. John Monteath
COACHES.
To EDINBURGH, the *Royal Mail* (from Dumfries), calls at the Spur Inn, every morning at nine; and returns for DUMFRIES at four in the morning.
To GLASGOW, the *Royal Mail* (from Carlisle), calls at the Beatock Bridge Inn, (two miles distant from Moffat, on the high road from Carlisle to Glasgow,) every morning at a quarter before nine ; and returns for CARLISLE at a quarter past one, going through Lockerbie and by Ecclefechan.
CARRIERS.
To ANNAN, Gavin Johnson and Jacob Richardson, every Friday.
To CARLISLE, Hargreaves & Son, twice a week. [Tuesday
To CASTLE DOUGLAS, Saml. Mounsie,
To DUMFRIES, James Johnston, James Robert Dickson, Samuel Mounsie, John Kilpatrick, & John Johnston, Tuesday.
To EDINBURGH, William Smith, John Proudfoot & Robert Baird, every Monday—James Johnston, Samuel Mounsie and James Robt. Dickson, every Thursday—and Andrew Smith, Gavin Johnston, and Jacob Richardson, weekly.
To GLASGOW, Hargreaves & Son, twice a week—and Samuel Scott & William Denham, once a fortnight.
To LOCKERBIE, Hargreaves and Son, twice a week, and Wm. Smith, Friday.

1800 In his book published in this year, Thomas Garnett provides an early account of the pleasant tiredness which often overcomes city-dwellers who come to Moffat:

> "Moffat has been long celebrated for its mineral waters, and on this account, numbers of invalids from Edinburgh, Glasgow, Dumfries, and various parts of Scotland, resort to it every year; and though in winter a residence here would be very dull and dreary, in summer the village is all life and bustle. The two inns accommodate a considerable number, and there are several private lodging-houses in which families can be accommodated. The climate of Moffat is said to be remarkably healthy, and the air so extremely pure, as to occasion sneezing and other marks of superoxygenation in persons not accustomed to it, particularly if they have lived for some time in a large town or confined situation: its effects are particularly exhilarating and bracing, as I have myself experienced; and though the showers of rain are frequent and sometimes heavy, as might be expected in a mountainous country, yet a moist or foggy atmosphere is seldom seen. Every opening of the clouds discovers a sky of a beautiful azure, which, in a clear day, assumes a distinctness and brightness that might vie with an Italian sky. These circumstances, with exercise, contribute, perhaps, as much as the waters to restore the exhausted and debilitated constitution." [130]

1801 James Hogg visited Moffat with Sir Walter Scott. The quality of the hospitality that they received fell a little short of the best but this seems to have added to the jollity of the occasion:

> "... Sir Walter, in the very worst paths, never dismounted, save at Loch Skene to take some dinner. We went to Moffat that night, where we met with some of his family (Lady Scott and Sophia), and such a day and night of glee I never witnessed. Our very perils were matter to him of infinite merriment; and then there was a short-tempered boot-boy at

the inn, who wanted to pick a quarrel with him, at which he laughed until the water ran over his cheeks." [131]

A COUNTRY RESIDENCE NEAR MOFFAT, TO BE LET

THE VILLA or COTTAGE, lately built at Heatheryhaugh, within a ſhort mile of the cheerful village of Moffat, and the like diſtance from it celebrated mineral waters – It contains the following accommodation:

Under Storey –   Kitchen, Scullery, two large apartments, and water-closet.
Principal Storey – Dining-room, Drawing-room, Library, and Butler's room.
Bed-room Storey – Four Bed-rooms and a large light cloſet.

The houſe is found and ſubſtantial, perfectly free from ſmoke, finiſhed in a plain and handsome manner, and furniſhed with neceſſary articles of the firſt quality – The external figure is fingularly neat, and the fituation peculiarly picturesque. Suitable Offices will be built as ſoon as the feason permits – Meantime feveral old buildings might ſerve temporary uſe.

About 24 Acres of incloſed and cultivated Land, and good Kitchen Garden, containing feveral full-bearing fruit trees, belonging to the premiſes, will be let in whole or in part with the houſe.

Application, by letter or otherways, may be made to Mr Syme, Dumfries.

Notice in *Dumfries Weekly Journal* 1803 [132]

1802 The Rev. John Brown came back to Moffat (despite his earlier encounter in 1787 with the dog) with his father:

"Another time - it was when his second marriage was fixed on, to our great happiness and his - I had just taken my degree of M.D., and he *(John's father)* took Isabella, William, and myself to Moffat. By a curious felicity we got into Miss Geddes' lodgings, where the village circulating library was kept, the whole of which we aver he read in ten days. I never saw him so happy, so open and full of mirth, reading to us, and reciting the poetry of his youth." [133]

1802 In October, two gentlemen went shooting from Moffat:

" ... and, after having killed a number of muirfowl *(grouse)*, hares, partridges, snipes etc. when one of the gentlemen descended a deep glen, within two miles of Moffat, a large beautiful young eagle sprung from one of the rocks. He happened to have a ball in one of his barrels (for the purpose of shooting deer) and with this he fired at the eagle and killed him. The eagle measured upwards of five feet from tip to tip of his wings. A few days before, a gentleman saw an eagle chased by two Roman ravens, near the same spot." [134]

Mrs. Middleton and her family, from Richmond in Surrey, were in Moffat:

> "... they arrived at Moffat, a small town, situated near two mineral springs, which attract many visitors for the sake of their medicinal qualities. From Moffat to Dumfries, the barrenness of the land and the poverty of the inhabitants rendered the ride unpleasant. The farm-houses are no better than miserable huts; and the people poor, and very dirty, the old women wrapping themselves up in a long cloak that reaches to the ground, with the hood drawn over their heads, and their legs defended only by huggers, or stockings without feet, which give them a wretched appearance." [135]

1804 "A Wanderer" made the journey from Lanark to Carlisle via Moffat. He and his companion had difficulty in finding suitable accommodation in the town but nevertheless they had nicer things to say about Moffat than Elvanfoot and Lockerbie:

> "Yet, wild and uninteresting as the scenery there was, it was far outdone by the still more dismal wilderness for the space of ten miles further, to the wretched habitation called an inn, at Elvanfoot; a second Mosspaul *(an inn between Langholm and Hawick)* in every respect, with the addition of uncivil people in the house. Here, unacquainted with its miserable state, we had determined upon passing the night: but a slight view of the place put all our former resolutions to flight; and though very unwilling to pursue our journey so far as to the next stage at so late an hour in the afternoon, there was no alternative.
>
> Accordingly we proceeded as soon as possible upon the way to Moffat, where we arrived sometime after it was dark. Here too, as if fortune was determined still to prosecute us, we could with difficulty procure most wretched accommodations for the night: the inns and every lodging-house in the town being full of travellers and persons stationary here upon account of the waters; the virtues of which have long been held in high estimation in scrophulous and scorbutic disorders, and supposed to be little inferior to those of Harrowgate in Yorkshire. Moffat is now increasing

much in size and opulence, in consequence of its being frequented by strangers; and it wears a flourishing and cheerful appearance.

The country in its immediate vicinity is pleasing and fertile; and the ride hence to Lockerby, through a part of Annandale, is picturesque, and agreeably diversified. Lockerby is a village of no importance whatsoever: it has an indifferent inn, and not a single building in it of any consequence." [136]

1805 Joseph Mawman had some interesting observations on the sartorial splendour of the inhabitants of Moffat:

"Moffat, we remarked, had much the appearance of an English town, from the number of people on the streets, and from their being generally, even on their lower extremities, well clothed. But our inquiries showed that these appearances were accidental: its populousness arose from their being two hundred and fifty invalids, who had come thither to enjoy a salubrious air and to drink the mineral water; the neat style of dress, from its being a particular day on which the inhabitants received the sacrament." [137]

1805 Robert Forsyth's account of Moffat gets off to an unpromising start but becomes warmer:

"The village of Moffat is only worthy of importance on account of its being a celebrated watering place. Though in a high country, it is pleasantly situated: it stands upon a rising ground, gently declining towards the south, to which the principal street looks, and hath a fine prospect of the valley below. It is encompassed on the west, north, and east, with hills of different heights, partly enclosed and cultivated, and partly in pasture. The street is wide and spacious, handsomely formed and gravelled, exceedingly smooth, clean, and dry in an hour after the heaviest rains, and is a most agreeable walk to the inhabitants, and to the company that comes for goats' whey or the mineral waters. The river Annan runs to the west of the village, at the distance of a few hundred yards, dividing a fine holm or valley, which is beautifully diversified by the windings of the river, the meadows, and corn fields. The plantations on all sides of the village are seen from the street, and every year appear with increasing beauty. There is one capital inn in the village, where the post-office is kept. There are other lesser inns, and several excellent lodging-houses, where the best company may be accommodated." [138]

1808 We will see that visitors arrived at Moffat using a remarkable range of conveyances but perhaps this is the most dedicated and difficult journey of them all:

"Willie Dalyell .... lived in Sanquhar. Willie was never married and his affection for his widowed mother was on one occasion exhibited in a remarkable manner. At the time the water at Moffat Well was highly spoken of for its healing virtues. To Willie it appeared to be the very elixir of life; if he could only get his mother to Moffat, there to get a drink of the wonderful waters, she would be restored to her former health and strength. But how was he to get her there? The distance was about thirty miles over the rough winding road among the high hills of Mennock and the upper reaches of the Clyde, and very seldom was there a cart going all the way.

Being too poor to pay for a conveyance, the prospect of the long tramp with an aged parent might be supposed to have deterred Willie from giving thought to this journey; but he was made of stuff that was not to be stopped by trifles. He did what perhaps no other man either before or since has done. He borrowed a stout wheel-barrow, placed his mother in it, and, wheeling her every foot of the way to Moffat, got her a drink of the well water, and trundled her back again. Unfortunately, all Willie's labour was in vain, for soon after this illustration of filial regard his mother went the way of all flesh." [139]

Beld Craig in 1800 [140]

1808 On 25th October the London Mail coach left the Trongate in Glasgow at 2.00 p.m. in a storm of gales and heavy rain. The driver, Alexander Cooper, and the guard, Thomas Kinghorn, had six passengers: Mr. Lund from London and Mr. Brand from Eccelefechan were on the outside while four others, a lady and three gentlemen, were inside.

About 10.00 p.m. that evening the coach drove on to the bridge over the Evan between Upper and Nether Howcleugh. The bridge, weakened by the spate of water, collapsed. The lady inside managed to scramble out and cling to a rock in the middle of the torrent from where she saw the lights of the approaching down mail. Her screams alerted the oncoming driver who sent to Moffat for help.

Mr. Lund and Mr. Brand were already dead, the three gentlemen from the inside of the coach were severely injured, the driver had a broken back and arm, and the guard had a severe head injury. Only the lady escaped unhurt having been rescued by the guard of the down mail, a John Geddes from Moffat. The story is that John lowered himself down the river bank with a pair of reins but then his modesty stopped him. "Whaur", he shouted, "will I grup her?". The lady heard and screamed in reply: "Grip me where you will, so you grip me tight."

Assistance eventually arrived from Moffat in the form of Mr. Clapperton, surgeon, and Mr. Rae, postmaster. Alexander Cooper died in Moffat about three weeks later and one of the other passengers survived after having his head trepanned by Mr. Clapperton. [141] [142]

1809 A fourteen year-old Thomas Carlyle and his friend Tom Smail walked from Ecclefechan to Edinburgh where they were to attend their new school. The journey took three days and they passed through Moffat on the way:

> "My Mother and Father walking with me, in the dark frosty November morning, through the village to set us on our way; my dear ever-loving Mother and her tremulous affection. But we must get to Edinburgh, over Moffat, over Eric-stane (Burnswark visible there for the last time)." [143]

1810 A French traveller described a scene with which we are all too familiar:

> "A few miles north of Moffat, the side of the hill over which we passed is worn away into a frightful chasm, called the Devil's beef-tub The view from the top must be very fine, but all was cloud and mist over the plain below, and we were left to fancy what we pleased." [144]

1810 John Finlay, the poet, was on his way from Glasgow to London when, on 8th December, he died from an apoplectic seizure at Moffat. John was only 28 years of age. We are told by his friend, John Wilson, that during his illness in Moffat he was "kindly treated by the worthy folk with whom he lodged. He was buried in the churchyard of Moffat - a beautiful village, which he especially admired, and in which the writer of this imperfect memoir had passed some delightful hours with him, in a pedestrian tour one year before." [145]

1810 Richard Philips published a recipe for bootleg Hartfell Water. The real thing is suddenly made more appealing:

> "For a natural imitation of the Hartfell water, first impregnate a pure water very slightly with iron and fixed air, in the common way, and to a quart of this water add one scruple of green vitriol, and alum three grains." [146]

1811 In about this year, two travellers spent a night in Moffat on their way from Carlisle to Glasgow. They were lucky enough to experience the passage of a drove of cattle which had probably come from the Highlands via Falkirk Tryst on its way to markets further south. The shortest route from Falkirk to England was via Lanark, Moffat and Carlisle and it came into Annandale down the Beef Tub at Ericstane:

"In our way through Moffat, we were much entertained by the arrival of a large drove of cattle, late in the evening, attended by many drovers with their bagpipes. This unexpected influx of national music, seemed to raise the spirits of the inhabitants: many parties assembled to dance to the sound of these strange but favourite instruments, and more than half of the night was expended before the sound of them ceased to disturb our rest: though disturbed however, the novelty and nationality of it, inclined us freely to forgive them." [147]

1815 In the summer of this year, an "English Commercial Traveller" made a journey south along the Evan Valley to Moffat. He observed the bridge which had collapsed, with loss of life, in 1808 and he was quick to jump to the conclusion that the lack of repair was due to local meanness:

"Between (Elvanfoot) and Moffat we passed over a bridge, through which the mail coach had fallen some years since. It was dark when we crossed it, but I could see the frightful chasm in the arch, which scarcely left room for a carriage to pass. The public spirited Scots will allow this to stand unrepaired till the remaining part of the arch falls in. They will then get Parliament to give them money to build a new one." [148]

1815 On 19th December Thomas Carlyle arrived in Moffat on top of the Glasgow Mail. He waited, probably in The Spur, for the coach to Edinburgh :

"In the hotel an English popinjay was amusing, being over-earnest about the details of feeding; and when he had monopolised the newspaper and was asked the news – "The Aachdoocs *(Archdukes)* have returned to England," said he, "and the Prince Regent is gone to Brighton." The snow was falling next day and the winds whirling it wildly as the

Edinburgh coach was struggling up past Erickstane. Carlyle and two Irish doctors got out and walked, the Irishmen delighted to reinforce by "outlandish warwhoops" the distracted bellowing of the coachman." [149]

1816 Dr. Samuel Heinrich Spiker from Prussia visited Moffat on his tour of England, Wales and Scotland. Dr. Spiker was Librarian to the King of Prussia. The house in Moffat which he describes as belonging to Mr. *Stevenson* may have been Larchhill, which was occupied at that time by Alexander *Stevens*. His impressions of Moffat were certainly better than those of Lockerbie:

"By Elvanfoot we reached Moffat near which the country becomes more picturesque. This bathing-place is much frequented; it is pleasantly situated in a hollow formed by the surrounding mountains, and although small, contains some rather elegant houses. The King's Arms inn, where we alighted, stands in the great place in the middle of the town, opposite to the theatre, where a play was to be performed on the following day *(the theatre was where Thomas Hetherington's shop now stands).*

In a walk through the town we came to the house of a Mr. Stevenson, distinguished from every other by its picturesque situation; from which we have a view of a great part of the town. A well-cultivated flower-garden in front of the house, added to the agreeable elegance for which it is indebted to its peculiar style of architecture, with a semicircular portico supported by four columns. There are several elegant houses, though none to be compared with this in the vicinity.

A walk to the Hartfell-spa, a sulphureous spring about two miles distance from the town, took us through an elegant avenue of birches and firs. The spring itself is covered over with a small house: a girl who opened it to us, gave us a glass of the water, which had a strong taste of sulphur. On our return, we met a great number of persons of all ages coming out of a Methodist chapel, in which we had before heard the preacher holding forth with great vehemence. At the inn there is a warm bath, and the water from the sulphureous spring may be obtained there in bottles.

The country between Moffat and Lockerby is as bare and desert as that at Moffat. We met considerable flocks of sheep, of which the herdsmen were all clad in the Scottish plaid, which is gray and striped. There are few inns in England so bad as that of Lockerby." [150]

1817 The Grand Duke Nicholas of Russia and his entourage stayed at the King's Arms (now the Annandale Arms Hotel) on the 8th and 9th of January and they were greatly impressed. The chamberlain, Baron Nicolai, paid double the bill on leaving, as the King's Arms was the only place they found in Scotland where the whole party had their own bed to sleep in. Mr. Robinson was landlord of the King's Arms at that time. [151] [152]

1817 In November, the comedian Charles Matthews was on his way from Glasgow to Moffat with two companions when the axle of their coach was damaged about seven miles from their destination. In driving wind, rain, sleet and snow, Mathews rode on one of the coach horses to Moffat where he sought the assistance of a blacksmith and then settled himself in:

"I reached Moffat in safety, drenched to the skin ... I put on some clothes of the landlord's and, in an hour after my arrival, was seated by a large fire, with a good beef-steak and some whisky punch." [153]

1817 A topographical account of Scotland offered the following description of Moffat:

"It is encompassed on all sides, except the south, by hills of different heights. The principal, or rather the only street, is spacious, with two good inns and lodging-houses, which are let to invalids during the summer. The church is a handsome building, surrounded with trees, which produce a good effect. The scenery around the village is delightful, and the salubrity of the air renders it an excellent place of summer retirement for invalids. Moffat has been long celebrated for its mineral waters." [154]

The King Arms in 1815 [155]

1820 In June, Anne MacVicar Grant, an American lady brought up in Albany, New York, took her daughter to Moffat to recover from illness. While in Moffat, Anne Grant wrote the following in a letter to her friend, Mrs. Smith:

"I think I shall, when the late fever of my mind has in some measure subsided, amuse you with some account of the place here. It pleases me exceedingly. The state of the poor, which always makes a part of my first concern when I come to a new place, is here very satisfactory. I feel miserable when surrounded with wretchedness that I cannot relieve; but the air of neatness and comfort here, even in the lanes and cottages, is balm to my worn-out feelings.

I daily pay a tribute of veneration to the benevolent spirit of the late good Earl of Hopetoun, to whom much of this order and comfort is owing. You must know that there is a considerable stretch of meadow-ground here, upon the banks of the Annan, which has long been accounted the common pasture of this little, neat, rural town. The rage for enclosing and improving has, however, reached even these green mountains and their pastoral dales; and the neighbouring farmers offered a great advance of rent for portions of this fertile meadow. But the Earl (blest be his bones) ordered that it should always be kept as a common grazing for the town, the inhabitants paying a very moderate consideration for this privilege. Sixty large, fat, full-fed cows make a respectable promenade, lowing through the streets, in the evening, as they proceed to their byres in the back lanes to be milked; and early risers, like myself, who live nearly twice as long as other people, witness their stately progress in the morning going out to their pasture. Much do I delight in the sight of these cows; the plenty they diffuse, and even the quantity of potatoes raised by their means, interest me .....

I continue my cart-excursions here with no small satisfaction. My companions are delightful, - the happiest, best, and most intelligent people imaginable. Their cart has such seats, and slings, and springs, as make it quite the king of carts; and the very horse is a sensible, well-behaved animal, worthy of your acquaintance." [156]

1822 In September, Dorothy Wordsworth (the younger sister of the poet William Wordsworth) visited Moffat with her friend, Joanna Hutchinson, and she was not enthusiastic about the town:

"... and from Lanark to Moffat in a cart. There stopped two days, my companion being an invalid: - and she fancied the waters might cure her – but the bathing-place which nobody frequents is never in order – a bath that *was* to have been warm proved worse than cold – and we were glad to leave Moffat." [157]

1823 Nathan Whitehead and a curate friend were in Moffat. The water definitely did not impress Nathan:

"We left Glasgow early in the morning in a post-chaise ... and after a long and toilsome day's travel, arrived in the evening at Moffat, where we remained a day. It contains some mineral springs, which are much celebrated in that part of Scotland. We walked out next morning to survey the town and taste the water, concerning the like whereof I had heard much, but never had the opportunity of tasting; but it is no way palatable to the taste, and my stomach loathed it mightily, and did so heave and twist itself that verily I thought my breakfast would have been of little service. But it was otherwise with the curate, whose stomach, he telleth me, is none of the kindliest; it sat lightly and pleasantly upon it, and did so animate and exhilarate his spirits, that he seemed, he informed us, as if he had drunk of the waters of Helicon." [158]

1823 Thomas Thomson, Professor of Chemistry at Glasgow University, came to Moffat to carry out yet another analysis of the well water. He also provided this general description of the town:

"The situation is rather beautiful, owing chiefly to the contrast between the bleak mountains constituting the background, and the finely wooded little hills and fertile fields in the immediate vicinity of the village. But the distant prospect is not so good. Annandale, which is stretched out immediately to the south, is too flat, and too bare of wood, to please the eye, and in point of culture seems rather behind the midland districts of Scotland. The mountains in Galloway and Cumberland are too low or too distant to form prominent objects, or relieve the flatness of the dale." [159]

1824 On 28th August Sir Walter Scott wrote from Drumlanrig to a lady who was about to visit him at Abbotsford:

"I came to this place yesterday by the road I propose *(via St. Mary's Loch and Moffatdale)*, and I found it capital good except about two miles which are rather rough but safe and practicable. There is a very decent inn called Betocks Bridge *(sic)* two miles on the Dumfries side of Moffat .... If you should determine to come by the Loughs you must appoint horses from Selkirk to meet you at the top of the Birkhill path where there is a shepherds hut *(Birkhill Cottage)* who can give you a tolerable breakfast of ham, eggs etc. but you must take a loaf or two of wheaten bread. You sleep at Betocks Bridge, and will get horses from there to carry you on to meet those ordered from Selkirk." [160]

1825 Mr. R. Abernethy undertook a walk, presumably for a large wager, from Colesworth, near Grantham in Lincolnshire, to Moffat. The total distance was 488 miles and he undertook to complete the distance in 7 days and 12 hours, or an average of 65 miles each day. He achieved this feat with 11 minutes to spare, taking twelve very painful hours to complete the final 26 miles. He did not comment on his no doubt brief visit to Moffat but this is hardly surprising since he must have been out of breath and in no mood to keep a journal. [161]

1825 Charles Green landed one of his hot air balloons at Wamphray on his way to Carlisle. This caused great excitement and people continued to flock to Wamphray for several hours after Charles had departed:

> "A knot of urchins who first beheld it, ran, calling out, "Mither, Mither, oh Mither! There's a great muckle thing fa'in frae the sky. It's nae angel but it's a glitterin' " (the sun was shining on the air ship). A boy who had been herding the swine of Mr. Carruthers of Hillhouse came running home... he seemed so terribly agitated that his friends actually thought that he had gone mad. He said that the "great muckle dragon" had come over the hill and lighted at the back of the stack-yard. By this time the whole countryside was astir and strangers flocked to the farm at Kilbrook." [162]

1826 On 27th August Sir Walter Scott made the trip from Abbotsford to the Grey Mare's Tail. He was probably not the first, and certainly not the last, to comment on the path:

> "To-day we journeyed through the hills and amongst the storms; the weather rather bullying than bad. We viewed the Grey Mare's Tail, and I still felt confident in crawling along the ghastly bank, by which you approach the fall. I will certainly get some road of application to Mr Hope Johnstone to pray him to make the place accessible. We got home before half-past four, having travelled forty miles." [163]

1826 Sir Walter recorded his drive from Yarrow down Moffatdale on his way to Drumlanrig. He stopped at Birkhill for a meal, and writes:

> "Our luncheon eaten in the herd's cottage; but the poor woman *(Jenny of Birkhill)* saddened me unawares, by asking for poor Charlotte *(Lady Scott, who had died about three months*

earlier) whom she had often seen there with me. She put me in mind that I had come twice over these hills and bogs with a wheeled-carriage, before the road, now an excellent one, was made. I know it was true; but, on my soul, looking where we must have gone, I could hardly believe I had been such a fool. For riding, pass if you will; but to put one's neck in such a venture with a wheeled carriage was too silly." [164]

1826 J. Erskine Gibson, a surgeon from Dumfries, had many good words to say about the health benefits of the town:

"Moffat is a handsome, smiling, little town, built upon rising ground, at the head of an extensive and romantic valley. Here are three good inns, and many excellent lodgings, which are let in summer to visitors, and invalids who repair hither for the benefit of the waters. The neighbourhood is sweetly pastoral, and abounds with delightful scenery.

The climate is particularly salubrious and the inhabitants seem to enjoy good health and sound constitutions, in a great degree. The atmosphere, notwithstanding the considerable quantity of rain which falls, is rarely moist or hazy, and the air is remarkably pure and keen; - so much so, that people who are used to the dense and smoky atmosphere of the larger towns, upon approaching Moffat, generally smell the great change, which is very bracing, enlivening the spirits, exciting the appetite, and not unfrequently occasioning, for the first two days, a slight catarrh, or discharge of thin fluid from the nostrils. These effects I have experienced more than once.

I consider Moffat, setting aside its wells, to be a most delightful summer residence; and I am convinced, that numbers of its visitors have derived more good from the purity of the air, change of company and diet, exercise, and amusements, than from the mineral waters to which it owes its celebrity." [165]

1826 It was in about this year that William Ritchie, the co-founder of *The Scotsman*, passed a few weeks at Moffat:

"Every morning he walked to the well, and occasionally bathed; and we well recollect the only convenience which he could obtain was an old barrel stationed in an outhouse, and filled with water carried in canfuls by the hands of the attendant." [166]

1827 Robert Chambers provides a pleasing account of the town although his description of the Grey Mare's Tail was unlikely to attract any visitors who were already prone to the occasional bout of melancholy:

"It is a delightful peculiarity of Moffat that many of its houses, as well as of the villas which surround it, are whitened. The whole place has thus a cheerful, cleanly aspect, very uncommon in Scottish villages. The town chiefly consists in a single spacious street, a great part of which is composed of handsome little boxes for the residence of the numerous invalids who annually flock hither ..... The environs of Moffat are remarkably beautiful, from the profusion of foliage occasioned by the ornamented villas.

The Grey Mare's Tail ... is the chief wonder of the south of Scotland in the department of the terrible and it is surrounded on every side by objects of a similarly wild and dread-inspiring character. A more terrible, more horrible, scene than this can scarcely be imagined; the precipice and falls are in themselves so terrible, and such is the depression of mind that takes place in these awful solitudes." [167]

1827 In July this description appeared in the *Caledonian Mercury:*

"Moffat is a remarkably neat clean village. The principal street is wide and spacious. It at one time contained two large inns, but at present there is only one of them is occupied. It is however one of most comfortable and moderate inns to be found in Scotland. The village is surrounded with beautiful walks, and there is in the neighbourhood abundant amusement not only for the sportsman, but for the antiquary, and the lover of the picturesque. Besides the inn there is an abundance of comfortable lodgings to be had at a moderate expense, and the produce of the dairy is to be had in great abundance and is very cheap." [168]

1828 In September Henry MacMinn of Lochfield, Dumfries, delivered a speech on *"The Beauties of Moffat and the Usefulness of That Excellent Mineral Spa"*. This extract is of interest for its observations on the recently opened Baths Hall. We should bear in mind that Henry's strength was in oratory rather than in prose:

"On my peregrinations to different watering-places, I visited a few days ago a small town called Moffat. For many years that town suffered a material loss in not having proper baths to accommodate the company who might visit that valuable well for their health, or even for amusement or pastime. I, as occasionally a visitor for nearly forty years and one who is very partial to Moffat, think it my duty to announce to the world in general that there are now erected, in a superior style in the middle of the town, and in a very wide spacious street, a number of as excellent and well-fitted up baths as I have ever seen, which reflect great honour on the public spirit of Moffat and its neighbourhood, and also on the architect for planning and building the said baths.

There are three different kinds of baths; the first are the baths of the Moffat water, the second are the artificial salt-water baths, third are the fresh-water baths, either warm or cold. The baths were all completely finished about three weeks ago." [169]

Annandale Arms Yard
Above the coach houses are the windows of the dining-room
which was also used as a ballroom.

87

1829 William Hare, of the infamous Burke and Hare, passed through Moffat. Hard working Irish immigrants by day, scheming murderers by night, William Burke and William Hare were a unique pair of criminals who made a profit from providing dead bodies to the anatomy students of 19th Century Edinburgh. Contrary to popular belief, Burke and Hare were not grave robbers: in fact there is no proof to suggest they ever robbed a single grave.

Hare, having turned King's evidence against Burke and Helen McDougal, was released from Calton Prison in Edinburgh on 5th February 1829. Using the alias Mr Black to confound the public, he left Edinburgh immediately. The authorities had arranged to return him to his native country of Ireland and they put him on the 9.15 p.m. mail coach to Dumfries from where he was to catch the Galloway mail coach to Portpatrick.

It has been suggested that Hare stayed in Moffat on his way to Dumfries but there is no evidence to support that idea. The 75 miles from Edinburgh to Dumfries took at least 8 hours at this time of year plus stops at the inn at Noblehouse (north of Romannobridge), the Crook Inn, and at other points on the route. The coach, with Hare aboard, certainly passed through Moffat but the stay at Moffat was limited, at most, to a stop to change horses and take on some refreshments. The Moffat coaching inn at this time was The Spur (now the Balmoral) but it is more likely that a stop was made at the Beattock Inn. It was still dark when Hare's coach passed through Beattock and it arrived in Dumfries at about 6.40 a.m. on 6th February. [170] [171]

What followed has been described as the "by far the greatest riot that ever occurred in Dumfries of modern date". The news of Hare's presence spread rapidly and a crowd, estimated at 8,000 people, gathered on the streets. The intention of many of the crowd was to "Burke him" by throwing Hare over the bridge at the head of Buccleuch Street. Through a series of subterfuges the authorities managed to get him out of Dumfries without any injury but he was taken to Carlisle rather than Portpatrick. The eventual fate of Hare is unknown although many popular tales tell of him as a blind beggar on the streets of London having been attacked by a lynch mob in Carlisle and thrown in a lime pit. However, none of these reports were ever confirmed. The last known sighting of him was in Carlisle. [172]

1829 Samuel Leigh wrote the following description of the town which contains at least one inaccuracy and a possibly unique reference to a "Peacock Inn":

"Moffat is a pleasant town, situated at the north extremity of Dumfries-shire, and at the head of the district called Annandale. It has long been famous for its sulphureous spring called Moffat Well, which is about one and a half mile distant. A good carriage-road leads from the town, and at the Well is a promenade-room, stabling, &c. At the end of the town, on the Dumfries road, near Evan Bridge, is a chalybeate mineral spring, but it is not resorted to.

The town stands in a delightful basin on the water of Moffat, and behind it runs the Annan. It consists principally of one street, the greater part of which is composed of lodging-houses, for the accommodation of persons frequenting the Wells. Most of the houses in the town and environs are whitewashed, and the whole has a very neat and clean appearance. Goats' whey may be obtained here in abundance. Population: 2,400. Inns: the Peacock; the Spur." [173]

Announcement in *The Scotsman* 1829 [174]

1829 This account of the Hartfell water would not cause the ordinary consumer to rush for the hills but it was written for a medical readership:

"This mineral spring is near Moffat, in Dumfriesshire, and contains iron, dissolved by sulphuric acid: it is very efficacious in scrofulous and cutaneous diseases ; and is used both internally and externally. When these waters are first used, they cause drowsiness, giddiness, and slight headache; but a gentle purgative will soon remove these symptoms. It is a good diuretic, and increases appetite. In ulcers of long standing, in those places where the texture of the diseased part is very lax, and the discharge excessive and ill conditioned, this water has acquired great reputation. The dose is less than that of most of the other mineral springs that are used medicinally. In delicate and irritable habits it is necessary to begin with a very small dose, as an over one will occasion griping and uneasiness in the intestinal canal. Besides, the Hartfell water is never used as a direct purgative. Few patients, even of the most robust habits, can bear more than an English pint of it in the course of the day: this quantity may be long continued. If the stomach of the invalid be very weak, it would be well to make the water tepid; and this process will not at all affect its medicinal properties." [175]

Announcement in *The Dumfries Times* 1834 [176]

1832 An unnamed correspondent came away with a pleasant impression of the town:

"This pleasing village ... is environed with lofty hills, some of them finely clothed in plantations of considerable beauty, an air of comfort and seclusion is therefore conveyed to the place, favourable to its character. One principal street, looking from the gentle declivity on which the town stands, towards the south, constitutes the body of the place, and affords fine prospects of the vale beneath. This street is judiciously laid out, spacious, and well calculated to form an agreeable promenade both for inhabitants and strangers.

Much of the town is new, and the whole has a neat, cleanly, appearance. Among the buildings are two good inns ... The town possesses upwards of fifty good lodging houses, whose private apartments may always be had on reasonable terms. The market is well supplied with provisions, including vegetables, fruit etc. Goats' and asses' milk is also to be had; and as there are more than a hundred cows kept in the parish, butter, milk, and cream are plentiful. Around Moffat are some neat villas, all of them adding more or less, by their shrubberies and small plantations, to the beauty of the scenery. The parish church is an ornamental structure in the place, and besides it there are several dissenting chapels." [177]

FOR SALE, BY PRIVATE BARGAIN,

THAT Large, Commodious, and Substantial DWELL-ING-HOUSE, AMOS PLACE, pleasantly situated in the immediate vicinity of MOFFAT, on the road leading to the well. The house is quite modern, and consists of Dining and Drawing-Rooms, Breakfast Parlour and 4 good Bed-Rooms, with Kitchen and Servant's Apartments, and every convenience, Stable and Coach-house, with an excellent Hay-loft and good Cellarage below. The ground extends to upwards of One Acre, is well inclosed and tastefully laid out, including Garden and Orchard well stocked. Such an excellent investment is seldom to be met with in this neighbourhood, as the village of Moffat, so long and deservedly famed, is rapidly improving; indeed, a more desirable residence for a genteel family seldom offers.
Sealed offers will be received by Mr MATHISON, the proprietor, addressed, Amos Place, post-paid, till 25th December, when, if not disposed of, will be exposed by Public Roup, on the First Friday of January, 1839, within the SPUR INN, here, betwixt the hours of eleven and one o'clock.
N.B.—There is excellent water on the premises.
Amos Place, Moffat, 24th Nov., 1838.

Notice in *The Dumfries Times* 1838 [178]

1832 Two sportsmen somehow found their way up Moffat Water and to Loch Skene. Like many before visitors before and since, Loch Skene had a peculiar effect upon their clarity of thought. Perhaps the whisky was to blame:

" .... thence to Moffat, and up that dismal glen, the pass of Moffat, to the Grey Mare's tail, a waterfall, so called from its resembling the silvery tail of a grey mare; and truly, if the simile were extended into infinitude, which from its sublimity it would admit of, we might compare its waving, silky stream swinging over the broad face of its lofty grey rock, to the tail of the pale horse of Revelation, over the chaos of time. It was a sombre, solemn sort of a day, and the dense clouds hung curtaining down the mountain sides, like our living pall as it were - I scarcely know how - but we felt dismally until we took a dram and got into a perspiration, with tugging up the sinuosities of the cliffs, to the summit of the waterfall.

Loch Skene, where we were galvanized, electrified, magnetised, and petrified, all at once, by the quackery, clackery, flappery, quatter, splatter, clatter, scatter, and dash-de-blash, and squash, of a flock of wild ducks, on its reedy, flaggy surface; O, what a scutter was there! Our hearts, too full, leapt into our mouths, but our guns were turned into tons of lead, and ere we could heave them up to our shoulders of clay, the thousand had fled into the eternal grey mist of the mountain, like the dispersion of a confused dream. There we stood like two sumphs, (as Hogg calls those who are ganging a bit agley in their wits) gaping and staring at each other with a look which said, why did not you shoot? Our dogs too stood as stiff as two pumps, with tails standing out like the handles!" [179]

1833 John Cairnie of Largs toured Scotland to compile a report on the state of the sport of curling:

"We find that at Moffat there are many keen Curlers; and from their proficiency in the game of Bowls, we conclude many of them can make a good use of the Channel Stane. There is a regular Club formed at Moffat, of which Thomas Jardine, Esq., is President. Perhaps from their rinks having been badly arranged, Moffat Curlers have not generally succeeded. They have been repeatedly beat by the parish of Kirkpatrick Juxta, although the population in that parish is less than in that of Moffat. The stones we saw in this quarter are not so well finished as those in use with us, and they generally run on one bottom." [180]

1833 Jane Welsh Carlyle and Helen Welsh visited Moffat, and Jane later recounted her memories:

"O Ellen! What a fearful recollection I have at this instant of your showerbathing at Moffat! It was indeed the sublime of showerbathing! The human mind stands astonished before it as before the infinite! In fact you have ever since figured in my imagination as a sort of Undine *(a water nymph)*." [181]

1834 The Rev. Dr. Singer, in writing about the Parish of Moffat, provided a Moffat's climate and healthy environment. At this time Dr. Singer was minister of Kirkpatrick-Juxta but for our purposes that is sufficiently distant for him to be regarded as a visitor:

"The climate and temperature of the village of Moffat may be stated most intelligibly by comparison, being neither so cold as in Edinburgh, nor so wet as in Glasgow; and not so warm as in Dumfries and Annan; but all observation and experience concur in assigning to Moffat a mild temperature, and a healthy climate. The town is built on, and surrounded by, lands of a dry and gravelly description, so that the streets and roads around the village are soon dried after falls of rain. It has a gentle declivity to the south, and a noble screen of lofty mountains protecting it from north and east, and frequently attracting showers which otherwise must have fallen in the vale. There is here no eastern fog or *haar* (as its is called in Edinburgh) when there is an east wind, nor is Moffat exposed to the dense fogs that visit and hang over Dumfries and Annan from the Solway Firth, and from the vast mass of spongy peat still undrained in Lochar Moss.

... the habits of early rising, in order to visit the well to which also there is a good walking and carriage road, have been thought materially to contribute to health. It may be added, that there is hardly any clay-bog undrained in the parish; that peat-bogs are not known to cause marsh fever; and that most of these are now drained for the benefit of the sheep, or for the purpose of being cut into peats, or improved and laid down in meadow grass; and, accordingly, among the residenters in Moffat, there are very few instances of ague *(any disease causing a fever)*. Typhus has often prevailed in Glasgow, Edinburgh, Carlisle, and other cities, when there was no such distemper in Moffat. Providence averted even the cholera, though severe in Glasgow, and especially in Dumfries, with which there was daily intercourse, - only two or three doubtful cases have occurred, and among strangers affected before they reached Moffat." [182]

1835 The Edinburgh mail coach overturned on the road from Moffat to Tweedshaws. The only passenger was so "under the thraldom of Morpheus" that he was unconscious of what had happened until he was dragged from the broadside of the coach. [183]

1836 A tourist guide contained the following account:

"The most wonderful scene in this district, and indeed in the whole southern part of Scotland, is the waterfall called the Grey Mare's Tail ... It is a truly sublime spectacle ... Here are no trees or flowers - artificial grottoes nor bridges - only the black rocks projecting over the bare mountain side. Passing through Craigieburn Wood, the tourist soon after leaves Dumcrieff and Oakrig on the left, and reaches the fashionable village of Moffat.

This place consists of one street, and the houses on either side are neat and clean. It stands at the bottom of a finely wooded conical hill, and is indeed surrounded by hills on all sides except the south. The river Annan skirts the west side of the town, and is joined below by the Moffat-Water on the one side and the Elvan-Water on the other. The village has long been famed as a watering-place, and, accordingly, the visiter will find good accommodation, with assembly-rooms, baths, bowling-green, &c. The well is at a little distance to the southward, as is also a cascade, called the Belle Craig.
The road from Moffat to Dumfries is almost totally devoid of interest; the only objects indeed, to be noticed, are, Raehill, on the banks of the Kinnel, the seat of Mr Hope Johnstone." [184]

1836   An unnamed correspondent came to report on the state of improved grassland in the area around Moffat. His prose does not flow freely but we get a good idea of his overall impressions:

> "I observed a great extent of improved pasture-land reaching high up the sides of the hills …. The fields are enclosed by stone-walls, as thorn hedges would not thrive in such situations. The dry spots of land within the new enclosures were broken up, and cultivated in the usual way. The land was then limed, and grass-seeds sown upon it, which completed the improving process. I was told the lime used was brought thirty miles, land-carriage, and the heavy expense of it, with that of the cultivation and seeding, incurred by the spirited and judicious occupiers, for the sole object of improving their pastures, without regard to corn-growing; I trust they live under liberal landlords and have long leases.

> Within the enclosures I saw fine Galloway bullocks, and Leicesters crossed with Cheviot sheep *feeding*, while, upon the unimproved land outside, the black-faced heath sheep were barely *existing*. That is an example worthy of imitation, and similar improvements may be effected in many other places, by the joint efforts of liberal landlords and spirited tenants.

> The Moffat enclosures are generally laid out in squares, and with their stone-walls have a stiff unsightly appearance in the landscape, being more unpleasant to the eye in picturesque scenery of undulating hill and dale. I, however, observed the woods and plantations in that district have been designed with better taste than in many other parts of Scotland." [185]

1836   A correspondent from *The Scotsman* gave a flamboyant account of the pleasures of Moffat:

> "This pleasantly situated and salubrious little village, around which Nature has so bountifully scattered her romantic graces, and upon which art has lavished so many ornate embellishments, is again gay as "a bridegroom who goeth forth to meet his bride". People from various parts

are daily dropping in, and the town has already assumed a considerable degree of its summer gayety; the invigorating air and healthful waters ever keep disease a stranger; and the fascinating society and endless diversity of amusements which abound, either tend directly to dissipate or stop the intrusion of rankling cares." [186]

1837 John Anderson's *Tourist Guide Through Scotland* was complimentary about the town but suggested one or two improvements:

"The village itself is pretty, and remarkably pleasing in its appearance; the street is spacious, and the houses whitened like an English village. A few years ago Baths were built and a reading-room, where the Edinburgh and London newspapers are daily received; and behind this is a bowling-green. But what is much wanted in the village is an ordinary *(an inn providing a meal at a fixed price)* for strangers. This ought to be immediately established, as well as a day-coach from Edinburgh, which would tend greatly to increase the influx of visitors to its mineral wells." [187]

1838 The Reverend Thomas Frognall Dibdin noted the quality of the accommodation in Moffat:

"We changed horses at Moffat, where there is a chalybeate spring, and where public rooms are built; and handsome lodgings may be obtained on moderate terms: the tiny Cheltenham of this northern domain, it is here the Edinburghers and Glasgovians equally resort, to kill grouse and time, and enjoy themselves by being miserable from want of employment. A little beyond, the ground rises sensibly, and for a considerable length carrying you to a height which a Southern might call mountainous. The road was incomparable.

The mail stopped to breathe the horses. It was close to the Devil's Beef-Tub, and the guard (the emperor of his species, for manly form and pleasant physiognomy) persuaded us to get out and look over the short wall which protects the passenger from falling precipitately into this smoking tub, and becoming one of the ingredients of its contents. I made a hurried sketch of it, which I could never afterwards lay my hand upon; but the scene is altogether as grand as peculiar."[188]

1842 William Howitt came through Moffat to explore the world of the poet James Hogg:

"To reach Ettrick, I took the mail from Dumfries to Moffat, where I breakfasted, after a fresh ride through the woods of Annandale. With my knapsack on my back, I then ascended the vale of Moffat .... But the pleasure of the walk ceased with the sixth milestone. Here it was necessary to quit Moffat and cross over into Ettrick dale. And here the huge hills of Bodsbeck, more villainous than the Brownie in his most vindictive mood, interposed. Preparing to set forward, what was my astonishment to see a cart and horse coming over the mountain with a load of people. It was a farmer with his wife and child, and they were about to descend the rugged, rocky, boggy, steep hill-side, with scarcely a track. They descended from the cart, the man led the horse, the woman walked behind, carrying the child, and they went bumping and banging over the projecting crags, as if the cart was made of some unsmashable timber, the horse a Pegasus, and the people without necks to break. 'Tis to be hoped that they reached the bottom somehow.

I had supposed by my map that from Moffat to Ettrick Kirk would be about six miles. Imagine, then, my consternation at the tidings these adventurous people gave me - that I had still eight miles to go! That, instead of six, it was sixteen from Moffat to Ettrick Kirk! There was a new road made all down this side of the mountain; very fair to look at in the distance, but infamous for foot travellers, being all loose, sharp cubes of new-broken whinstone." [189]

MOFFAT.—A numerous company of farmers and tradesmen met in Mr Charters' Star Inn here, to do honour to the coronation of our youthful Sovereign, Queen Victoria. There was a splendid ball in the pump-room (which was brilliantly lighted with gas for the first time,) where all went " merry as a marriage bell " till an early hour of the following morning, when the festivities terminated in joyful harmony.

The Scotsman 1838 [190]

1846 About 7,000 men were employed to construct the Caledonian Railway and at one point the number of navvies, their wives and children in the Lockerbie to Beattock Summit section approached 1,500. The conditions of work were appalling. Many of the navvies suffered from scurvy and there were frequent severe injuries and deaths. The full story of the navvies in the Moffat area remains to be told elsewhere but drunkenness, particularly on pay-day, gave rise to the following account which is perhaps apocryphal:

> "One of the navvies had spent several days in the village *(Moffat)*, drinking the remainder of his month's pay, and when satisfied he had melted his last shilling, he was returning to join his work, and had proceeded several miles on the road, but putting his hand into his pocket, he discovered that he had still 1s. 6d. remaining – he started as if he had put his hand upon a snake, as he knew his unhappy propensity would not allow him to return to work till it was spent; so he accordingly retraced his steps, drank the remaining 1s. 6d. with all possible despatch, and then set out peaceably and commenced work with a satisfaction peculiar to himself." [191]

The Grey Mare's Tail [192] [193]

1846 Thomas Carlyle certainly was not impressed by the habits of the navvies. He had visited Moffat in the autumn of 1846 and the following year, in a letter to a friend, he reported unfavourably on his visit:

"Last autumn I was two days at Moffat: they are tearing up the whole country there; carrying their railway from Carlisle and London thro' the Evan valley, towards Glasgow and Edinburgh: to be open as far north as Beattock in August next, they say. The Country was redolent of more whiskey and blackguardism, every village (Moffat among others) full of drunk Navvies; not pleasant to see!" [194]

1847 This extract from an item in *Tate's Magazine* provided a vivid summary of the terrors of Ericstane Brae. However the author was clearly no authority on the estimation of the heights of hills:

"Hartfell, in the upper part of this country, rises to the height of 1,928 feet above the level of the sea; and several individual heights of the same group approach very near to that elevation. The pass of Errickstane Brae from Dumfriesshire into Tweeddale is very steep and tedious, even with the present improved line and construction of road ; but in the olden times, and when wild forests prevailed everywhere over the sides of the hills, and darkened the depths of the valleys - and when these were most likely to be peopled by robbers - one cannot doubt that the good Catholic would gladly avail himself of the cross at

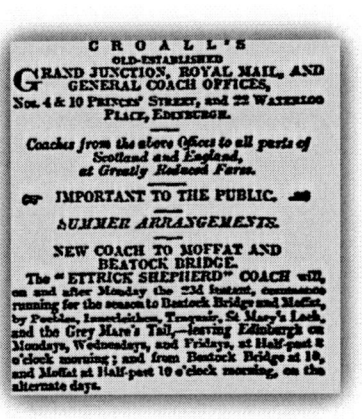
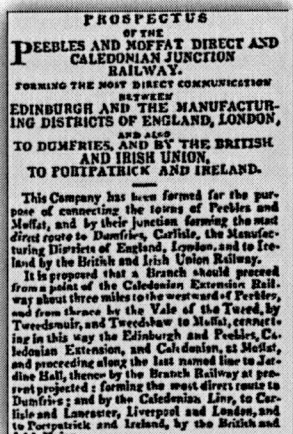

Announcements in *The Scotsman* 1845 [195] [196]

the summit, to throw himself upon his knees, and offer up fervent prayers for his safety. In these times, the traveller's attention is arrested by a most remarkable conchoidal hollow, in the bosom of the mountain, of immense depth, with sides of a declivity approaching nearly to the perpendicular, covered with a beautiful short green sward. This very curious place is called "the Marquis of Annandale's Beef Stand", - probably because its quiet shelter, and rich pasture, may have produced very superior beeves." [197]

1848   In July, William Wallace Fyfe wrote about his visit to Moffat and his fond recollections are worth quoting at some length:

"Here we are, however, at Beatock where Mrs. Holmes keeps one of the neatest tables ever spread, in the refreshment rooms, and one of the most enticing inns, in the vicinity. The Beatock Inn is very much frequented, and presents highly superior accommodation. The best introduction to Moffat itself is to be obtained inside the omnibus, where the stranger learns that a list of all the let and unlet lodgings may be seen at the shop of Mr. James Stewart, bookseller.

Arrived at Moffat, the stranger finds its brilliantly whited houses nestling amongst the new and thriving wood which climbs up the beautifully laid out steep of the Gallow-hill. Since the sanitary conditions of towns have attracted so much attention, one is always suspicious. But nuisances in

Moffat are so carefully interdicted, that, in looking into the back settlements, we believe it would be difficult to trace anything beyond the ordinary accommodation for the cow, which every villager of Moffat has the privilege of sending to the common *caar*.

Of the company at the Well many may certainly be seen there drinking for health; some in the period, but not the bloom, of youth, struggling to attain a miserable age; others already old, making the vain effort to renew their youth; but the majority are manifestly drinking for pleasure, or, at least, to scare away even the anticipation of pain. The "Long Room" used to be laid out under the auspices of Mrs. Cranstoun, for public breakfasts, of which there were 80 or 100 very frequently every morning, followed by a dance upon the external turf." [198]

1848 An unnamed correspondent made some very favourable comparisons between Moffat and two of its rival spas: Harrogate, and Wildbad (now Bad Wildbad) in Germany. This piece provides some interesting information on the standard of accommodation for visitors to Moffat. We should skip lightly over the stereotypical insinuations of Scottish meanness:

"Economical Scotchmen, reading Dr. Granville's works on the spas [199] .... wherein he takes up the comparison betwixt the extravagant charges at the fashionable spa hotels of this country, and the comparatively moderate rates of the same class abroad would be panic-struck at the doctor's notions of moderation, even as illustrated in Germany.

In treating at Harrogate, he estimates the weekly expense of a gentleman and his lady, with three daughters, and two men and a woman servant, living at one of the principal hotels, and using the public room, at not less than 23 guineas a week. The same number of persons would, he said, have been magnificently lodged, and sumptuously fed, in the new hotel at Wildbad, called "The Bellevue", for 18 guineas a week.

We can tell the doctor a secret: it is, unless a man were utterly fey or daft, his family expenses at a Scotch watering place could hardly by possibility exceed a tithe *(a tenth)* of the latter sum; more especially is this the case at Moffat, where expensive and monopolising hotels are not tolerated, but everything is done upon a public principle, both at the baths in town, and the well upon the mountain, which insures the exaction of the most trifling, and indeed, nominal charges, from all ranks and classes. The accommodations, it is true, bate something of southern splendour; but the visitors, though nothing averse to elegance, if they can secure it, are generally content to prefer comfort and quiet, as much more suitable to their purpose than all the magnificence in the world.

.... the veterans of Moffat point with pride to some ruinous huts on the Old Well Road where, in days of yore, "a lord once slept", which certainly seem anything but aristocratic now. My own experience of lodging-hunting was brief ... I found my choice limited to some dark and low apartments, on the ground floor of a little cottage in the outskirts, or a more circumscribed eyrie in one of the back street of the town, at a third part of the rent. The moderation of the terms astonished me beyond measure. I had never found at any other watering-place the same amount of convenience and, as it proved, attention, to be had for the money." [200]

1849 An unnamed correspondent and his companions walked from Tibbie Sheil's to Moffat. They visited Loch Skene on the way where they had a profound metaphysical experience:

"We have subsequently visited York Cathedral, one of the proudest fanes of these islands but its vaulted roofs, "its long-drawn aisles", its "dim religious light," evoked no sentiments so awful, so solemn, so memorable as the temple of Loch Skene.

We rose slowly from the posture of devotion, looked somewhat dreamily around, and, found ourselves, in a state of utter exhaustion, slowly pursuing our way to Moffat, which we reached at a late hour, after having spent a day that shall never be forgotten in the annals of our moral and religious history." [201]

A GOOD EXAMPLE.

TO THE EDITOR OF THE TIMES.

Sir,—As a contrast to the charges of Mr. Cox Hughes at the Brunswick I enclose the hotel bill at Beattock-bridge, on the Caledonian line, paid by two ladies, now on a visit at my house, with an account of their fare and treatment while there.

Beattock is a very convenient stopping place for travellers, coming from the South to Perth, Montrose, or Aberdeen, and I think Mr. Ramsay deserves encouragement.

I am, Sir, your constant reader,
Brotherton Bervie, N. B.　　　　DAVID SCOTT.

Breakfast		3 4
Tea		3 0
Lodging		2 0
Servants		1 0
		9 4

Two ladies, on arrival per rail from the South, were conveyed in a carriage from the station (and back next morning), had tea, with broiled ham and eggs, a double-bedded room at night, breakfast next morning, with broiled salmon and eggs, and were again conveyed to the station. The whole charge for everything mentioned above, and attendance likewise, was 9s. 6d.

The fare and accommodation were alike good, and the greatest civility and attention were shown by the attendants.

Letter to *The Times* 1849: [202]

1849 James Hogg (the poet's son) took a three-day trip with friends from Edinburgh via Peebles to Birkhill and Moffat and then back to Edinburgh. They walked the full distance of the leg between Peebles and Moffat. Having enjoyed good hospitality at Tibbie Sheil's and at the Birkhill howff, they stopped for a cool bath in the pool at the foot of the Grey Mare's Tail before walking on down through Moffatdale:

"Like Innerleithen approached from Peebles, no signs of a town are visible until a sharp turn of the road discloses it all at once lying before you, sweetly nestled amongst the surrounding hills. Like Innerleithen, also, it boasts of its mineral well - at present said to be rather more the rage than those of poor St Ronan's; but we had seen and drank enough of water for a time, and were, besides, in very proper condition to feel - not as Byron has it, "the strong necessity

103

of loving," but of eating. A handsome hotel, "The Annandale Arms", was therefore more to our taste.

After a ramble round the town, we waited patiently for the arrival of the vehicle which was to bear us home. The mail drove up in good time, and we prepared to take our seats as a matter of course; but what was our consternation to discover that not one seat was empty - that the mail had been full freighted from Dumfries - and that there was no other conveyance till next day! Here was a pretty fix! In town *(Edinburgh)* we must be next morning, at all hazard - but how? Our feet could scarcely carry us one out of the fifty miles necessary to be traversed, and yet there seemed no other alternative. While looking about, the images of despair, we were accosted by two other unfortunates in exactly the same position; urgent business requiring their presence in Edinburgh next morning. We now talked magnificently about a post-chaise, and were just about to order the vehicle, when it was discovered that the joint funds of the three would not cover the expense of one for this mode of conveyance.

Another dilemma! But a good angel came to our relief. A gentleman had been standing on the door-steps, listening to our conversation, who now quietly turned round to one of our number and said – "' What money do you want?" – "Why," said the person addressed, "you don't propose giving money to utter strangers, of whom you know nothing, and whom you may never see again." - "Oh, I have no fears," was the reply, "mention the sum, and you shall have it." Here was romance in these money-grubbing times; so not to disappoint the gentleman of his eccentric generosity, we accepted from him a considerable loan, and politely invited him to join us in some refreshment in the inn - which, however, to the everlasting scandal of our memory, we left our generous friend to pay - a pretty recompense for his kindness!

The Caledonian Railway, now finished, passes within two miles of Moffat, and coaching on the road is consequently at an end. With coaching disappears all the romance of travelling, and we may thus regard the excursion just detailed as among the last of the pleasurable free-and-easy journeyings which are likely to be enjoyed on this line of road. But substantial advantages remain. Our party, in addition to anxiety and loss of time, were mulcted in rather more than one pound sterling each for a distance which may now be travelled at the cost of one-fifth part of this sum." [203]

Front Page from the First Edition of
The Moffat Register & Annandale Observer

THE

Moffat Register & Annandale Observer.

No. I.	SATURDAY, 4TH JULY, 1857.	ONE PENNY.

Moffat Register & Annandale Observer.

SATURDAY, 4TH JULY, 1857.

MOFFAT has a celebrity of nearly three centuries as a watering place. In point of scenery, salubrity, and situation, it is unsurpassed by any summer residence in Scotland. " Its walks and its wells" are extensively famous, and many of the noble, the learned, and the good, have dwelt, for longer or shorter periods, within its borders. In the natural progress of society greater variety of scenery and change is now accessible, even to the middle classes, than was attainable a few years ago. Though competition has thus been stimulated, Moffat still retains a high place among the Spas of our country: it annually attracts crowds of visitors, and contributes to their health and enjoyment. We cannot doubt that curiosity to know something of those scenes in which they for the time reside, extensively prevails among our visitors, and that they are often anxious to have some record of the doings which take place within it, that they may gratify their friends by laying before them the manner of the life of those who permanently reside in it. Such a desire it is presumed "THE MOFFAT REGISTER" would content.

The Press has recently had new duties placed before it; has had its range widened, and its capacity for good enlarged. It has now—taking all its appliances together—become one of the mightiest agencies for the spread of civilization. No civilization can be adequate to the necessities of man except such as shall lead him to live in truer brotherhood and closer harmony of feeling, thought, and interest, than heretofore with his fellows. The idea has long been fixed in the mind of the present writer that Literature has not yet been sufficiently *domesticated* in our country—that it has hitherto been too political, too much kept

apart from the sympathies which man should have for man—too much concerned with the State, the Parliament, war, the law courts, and the crimes of cities, and too inattentive to the culture of a true, kindly, Christian feeling of *neighbourhood*, and a genuine desire for mutual co-operation in the effectuation of good.

It is presumed that Moffat is specially fitted for initiating an attempt so to domesticate literature, by producing in it a periodical which shall—so far as space permits—combine within itself a local news journal, a friendly visitor, and a medium for communicating such details regarding Moffat and its vicinity as may be pleasing to the visitor and interesting to the resident. Such a periodical the present aims at becoming. It will contain such local news as may seem likely to be useful or agreeable, carefully subordinated to the preservation of the purity and integrity of the home circle; such general intelligence—specially abridged and collated—as is worthy of, and suitable to family perusal; such biographies, historical and topographical sketches, as may appear to be of general interest, conducive to the advancement of society in morality, intelligence, comfort, or religious feeling or action, or capable of adding the beauty of association to the natural scenic loveliness of Moffatdale and Annandale.

We make the present number before our readers as an experiment in what we regard as an important literary development. If they decide that it is likely to suit their taste and gratify their wishes, we shall continue our task; if not, we shall withdraw from the endeavour, disheartened indeed, but not despairing. We ask no reward except the power of doing some good in our generation. Let Moffat be so just as to give us a fair trial—forbearing to decide too hastily upon an experiment requiring time, experience, talent, and research for its due adjustment and conduction—and we dare venture

to promise that our efforts shall not be altogether unworthy of their favour. We abjure all intention of meddling with political or public affairs, except when the cause of home society and religion seem to call upon us to say our " word in season: " when such a contingency arises we shall be at our post, vigilant watchers, to say that word with fearlessness, candour, and charity, honestly striving to do the work of our day, in an humble reliance on the power of Christian truth, to effect the high purposes of domestic and social regeneration. *S. Neil*

LOCAL NEWS.

THE COMMUNION.—This sacred ordinance will be celebrated in our parish on Sabbath, 26th inst., the Thursday previous being, as usual, observed as a day of humiliation and prayer.

EPISCOPAL CHURCH SERVICE.— On Sabbath first (to-morrow), 5th July, religious worship, according to the forms of the Church of England, will be conducted in Morison's School, Well Road. Diets : 11 forenoon and 6 evening.

VISITORS continue to arrive by most of the trains. A list of such as we could conveniently get the names of we have presented in another column. We hope that, in an experimental issue like the present, allowance may be made for omissions or errors. The haste and bustle of a first number plead for us.

THE BAND.—It will be pleasing to present, as well as intending visitors, to learn that the committee who have charge of these arrangements have completed their task, so far, at least, as to engage a most excellent staff of musicians, able to use both wind and stringed instruments we hear, under the leadership of Mr. F. S. Busbee of Glasgow. A programme of their intended proceedings will be found in another column, and we have no doubt, be considered highly satisfactory.

THE WEATHER.—The rain-fall of the month ending June 30, was 2.9 inches. The chief portion of this fell in the early days of the month. The average heat of the whole month of June was 54.46 degrees.

THE WELL.—During the week the "Well" has been much frequented. The various parties seemed to enjoy their early morning walk, their cooling draught, and their merry meeting.

GAS.—The Gas Company are most praiseworthily extending their operations. They intend not only to improve the light, but also, we believe, materially to reduce the present rate. These shares are guaranteed to yield, at least, 5 per cent. All who can should invest.

106

Advertisements from *The Moffat Register* 1857 - 1859

Moffat Railway Act 1882

CHAPTER xlviii.

An Act to enable the Moffat Railway Company to construct a railway to the Beattock Station of the Caledonian Railway Company and for other purposes. [19th June 1882.]

A.D. 1882.

WHEREAS by the Moffat Railway Act 1881 (in this Act called "the Act of 1881") a company (in this Act called "the Company") was incorporated and authorised to make and maintain a railway in the county of Dumfries described in that Act and was authorised to raise a share capital of sixteen thousand pounds and to borrow five thousand three hundred and thirty pounds :

44 & 45 Vict. c. lxxxii.

And whereas it is expedient that the Company should be authorised to make and maintain the railway herein-after described and to raise further share capital and to borrow further moneys :

And whereas it is expedient that the Company and the Caledonian Railway Company should be empowered to enter into and carry into effect working agreements :

And whereas plans and sections showing the line and levels of the railway together with books of reference to such plans containing the names of the owners or reputed owners lessees or reputed lessees and of the occupiers of the lands and property required or which may be taken for the purposes of or under the powers of this Act have been deposited for public inspection in the office of the principal sheriff clerk of the county of Dumfries and are herein-after referred to as the deposited plans sections and books of reference :

And whereas the purposes of this Act cannot be effected without the authority of Parliament :

May it therefore please Your Majesty that it may be enacted and be it enacted by the Queen's most Excellent Majesty by and with the advice and consent of the Lords Spiritual and Temporal and Commons in this present Parliament assembled and by the authority of the same as follows :—

1. This Act may be cited for all purposes as the Moffat Railway Act 1882.

Short title.

[*Local.—48.*]   A   1

The Moffat Railway

On 10th October 1862 John Miller, an engineer from Edinburgh, presented a scheme for the Moffat Railway to a public meeting in the Baths Hall. The estimated cost was £7,500 - £8,000. The meeting unanimously resolved that the line should be built but in December 1862 the proposal was abandoned due to opposition from many inhabitants and from John James Hope-Johnstone, and lack of interest from the Caledonian Railway. The scheme rumbled on until the Moffat Railway Acts of 1881 and 1882 enabled the raising of share capital of £16,000 and the borrowing of £5,330 to finance the project.

Miss Hope-Johnstone cut the first sod on 13th December 1881 but construction was delayed by the need to cut through hard whinstone. The line was 1 mile and 71 chains (3,038 metres) in length. The single line left the up side of the main line at milepost 40 north of Beattock and was carried over the Evan Water by a brick arch with freestone piers, 35' in span and 25' high. It then passed beneath the Glasgow - Carlisle road, 150 yards north of Beattock Hotel, at a depth of 18' and ran level across the fields opposite Lochhouse Tower to the spur of Coates Hill, where there was a cutting 176 yards long and 25' at its deepest point. The Dumfries Road was crossed by a skew bridge with freestone piers and malleable iron girders 25' high. The line then went through the Dyke Meadow, with a falling gradient of about 1:71 for about 900 yards, until it reached a point nearly opposite Langshaw House where the gradient rose about 1:105 for about 300 yards to a bridge over the Annan. This bridge was of freestone with iron girders 43' 3" span, and 8' above the water. From here the station was a level run of 440 yards.

John Wood, from Carlisle, was the engineer for the project; A.B. Smith the resident engineer; A.H. Boyle, from Hamilton, the contractor for the line; and Messrs Kinnear, Moodie and Co. of Edinburgh the contractors for the station buildings, goods shed, and signal cabins. The first train, on 2nd April 1883 at 7.30 a.m., was busy but it was not until the afternoon, when the town's shops were closed, that the station was filled with a large number of people. From 3.00 p.m. trips on the train were free and the carriages were packed. At 3.30 p.m. cake and wine were served in the station waiting room to a large company of ladies and gentlemen.

The 'bus fare from Moffat to Beattock had been 6d. for a single journey but by rail it cost only 2d., or 3d. for the return journey. There were also savings in parcel rates. The railway trip took only six minutes, compared with about 13 minutes. The omnibus service between Moffat and Beattock was discontinued immediately and the vehicles now plied between the station and the town. Moffat Station was licensed for the sale of wines and spirits and it boasted a John Menzies bookstall.

MOUNTAINS AS SEEN FROM THE TOP OF COATES HILL

North

East

West

1 *Coatehead Hill*
2 *Hartfell*
3 *Birnock Cleves*
4 *Well Hill*

5 *Gallow Hill*
6 *Hydropathic Estab.*
7 *Deil's Beef Tub*
8 *Bodsbeck Law*
13 *Craigour*

9 *Lochfell*
10 *Craigbeck Hope*
11 *Frenchland Tower*
12 *Queensberry*

from Fairfoul's Guide to Moffat 204

110

1850   The Rev. Thomas Grierson visited Moffat and he was enthusiastic about the town, although he was not complimentary about the habits of its visitors:

"There is no town in Scotland better aired, or more clean and tidy, than Moffat. The principal street is unusually broad, and contains many excellent lodging-houses, with neat shops in the under-storey; and the neighbourhood, especially towards the Well, is ornamented with tasteful villas and cottages, the very *beau ideal* of snugness and comfort.

The general style of building in Moffat is peculiar, and has a very substantial and pleasing appearance. The hard compact stone natural to the district, being coarsely polished, squared and oiled, has a dark grey aspect, and contrasts agreeably with the white sandstone ribbets at the corners and around the windows. But if the exterior is becoming, in almost all instances the interior is equally so, as the inhabitants vie with each other in making their lodgings as handsome and commodious as their respective means will admit – even the lowest-prices among them being vastly superior to cottages of similar dimensions in other places, while the inmates are particularly civil and obliging.

As regards their *(the waters of the Well)* medical pretensions, I profess myself much of a sceptic, being firmly convinced that good, common, mountain water is, in every respect, preferable to them all. My conviction is that the quantity of water imbibed by visitors would, in many instances, be most injurious, were it not for the exercise and variety in which they are accustomed to indulge when removed from their usual places of residence.

The reading-room, billiard-table, and bowling-green, are the three principal attractions of that description to Moffat loungers; but let men do what they will at such places, time, I suspect, still hangs heavy on their hands during certain portions of the day, owing to the want of their customary regular employment. Reading is seldom resorted to much purpose by water drinkers, any more than by Oxonians and Cantabs, who, under the imposing term reading, think of little else than amusement, when they retire from their colleges to Wales or the Lakes. The bowling-green seems in very good order; but it has often surprised me that it should be so little used.

Of late years, the Well has been much improved by a handsome pavilion, open at one side, in which dancing might be practised under very interesting circumstances; the music being accompanied by the bleating of lambs, the crowing of grouse, and the "wild bravura" of the curlew. Here I cannot omit drawing particular attention to the extremely neat apartments - a sitting-room and two bedrooms - belonging to the tenants of the Well. The rooms are small, but very comfortable, and the young couple who possess them seem amiable and obliging.

The drive to the Grey Mare's Tail is the favourite pastime of Moffat visitors, and so fashionable has it become, that the worthy hostess of the Annandale Arms has erected stabling for her horses near the foot of the fall. It is gratifying to think that this season, so far as it has gone, has, in posting, proved more than usually profitable to that enterprising lady." [205]

1850 In October the *Dumfries and Galloway Standard* published this story, from an informer in Moffat, of a romantic interlude. Newspapers nowadays would surely publish the names of the parties involved but more is the shame. We trust that both elopers managed to live happily ever after and that their memories of Moffat were eternally happy ones:

"Our community has been thrown into a state of excitement by the elopement of a young lady, daughter of Mr. ----, a member of one of the learned professions in Edinburgh, who, with his family, has taken up his winter residence in one of the neat villas at Well Road, Moffat. It would seem that the bold Lothario, who appears to be a very young man, with a military cast in his habiliments, had been for some days concocting measures for the issue that has now been arrived at; for on the night of Wednesday last, a conveyance

112

was ordered from Mrs. Cranstoun's *(the Annandale Arms)* to convey a party to the mail train due at Beattock at 10.41 p.m.

The conveyance was ordered to remain at a distance from the lady's residence, the gentleman keeping watch and ward over it, while the driver, acting under instructions, went for sundry pieces of luggage, which were concealed among the fine shrubbery which the taste of the proprietor has planted round the house. The luggage and lady being duly deposited in the conveyance, they were driven to Beattock station and booked for Carlisle, and "were o'er the border and away" before the lady's absence was discovered. The lady's personal attractions are of a very high order. The last thing heard of the happy couple is that they are in Liverpool, where it is supposed arrangements had been made for their marriage."[206]

1851 The philosopher and angler Robert Blakey, in his best-selling book about fishing in the rivers and lochs of Scotland, demonstrated a sensitive appreciation of the environment which is so often displayed by anglers:

"The Moffat Water .... flows down the narrow valley between St. Mary's Loch and Moffat, and has a connexion with Loch Skene by means of the Grey Mare's Tail burn. There is good trouting in the Moffat Water, but I have never seen very large ones taken out of it. It is a pleasant stream to angle with a single-handed rod; and its banks and windings among the high hills have a solemnising and contemplative effect upon the mind. If the angler ascends the stream till he comes to the rivulet that leads up to the Grey Mare's Tail, he will be much interested. This glen forms an immense cliff between two high mountainous ridges, running from cast immense cliff between two high mountainous ridges, running from cast to west. The descent from either side is steep and rugged in the extreme.

The valley is very narrow through which the Moffat makes its way, with many abrupt windings. The river is stretched out like a silver thread as we cast an eye down the vale from any of the surrounding hills. For a considerable distance, the vale does not average more than two or three hundred yards in width; and the whole scene often recalls to the mind the Vale of Tempe, so graphically described by Lillian. There are here, however, no smoking altars of incense - no thickets overshadowing the sides of the stream, to screen the weary traveller from the rays of the sun - no convivial parties enjoying themselves in sequestered groves - no musical birds warbling among the green branches of the ivy-mantled trees, described in the celebrated defile between Ossa and Olympus; but, notwithstanding all this, the glen is a scene which, for simplicity and grandeur, cannot easily be rivalled, and the tourist who has once passed through it will not soon forget it." [207]

1852 The following is an extract from an article which appeared in the *Scottish Guardian*, a literary review published in Glasgow and edited by William Keddie who was a particular lover of Moffat:

"We might search broad Scotland in vain for a spot encircled by a greater variety of attractive objects than the little village of Moffat .... One is struck everywhere about Moffat with the freedom of access which is afforded to places of interest. There are no *affiches* on the trees and walls threatening transgressors with the rigours of persecution, or giving mysterious token of the presence of spring-guns and mantraps." [208]

1852 Lydia Ann Barclay, a Quaker minister, visited Moffat:

"I was mercifully enabled in peace to leave Edinburgh the next day, and go to Moffat, a quiet little watering place among the mountains of the border country towards Carlisle, where dear J. and H. H. came to us, and we enjoyed a sort of feast of unity and sympathy and love, which was truly strengthening, as well as cordial and reviving to us .... They very much enjoyed the Scottish beautiful scenery, and so did we, and felt the better for the thorough change .... We left Moffat with much regret on seventh day last." [209]

1852 Another contribution to this year was from John McDiarmid, the editor of the *Dumfries Courier*. He was one of the best-known editors in Scotland at the time but he also appears to have had a prodigious talent for flowery language:

"It is true that Moffat, irrespective of its character as a watering-place, is only a village, trending upon a market town, situated on the skirts of an extensive sheep country; and remains to this day undistinguished by the usual appendages of town-house, jail, burgesses and incorporations, which denote the existence of a royal or baronial burgh. And hence the presence of many virtues and the absence of not a few vices - the spawn, so to speak, of political jobbing and contested elections. How often, under the olden system, and in the case of the smaller burghs, has a royal charter produced all the effects of the upas tree, drying up the sources of moral purity, and blasting and withering everything around. How often have gains, equivocally come by, palsied the very hands that clutched them, unnerving the arm of manhood, and planting wrinkles prematurely on the brow - depopulating the workshop, and peopling the tavern - stilling the anvil's din, the shuttle's play, and identifying every croft with the possession of the sluggard. Be thankful, then, my favourite Moffat, that you possess attractions worth a hundred royal charters. Thy wells are not only pure in themselves, but the medium of purity is everything else." [210]

1853 In July, Jane Welsh Carlyle was staying at Moffat House when she visited the Grey Mare's Tail. She should have known what to expect there because her mother, Grace Welsh, was from Caplegill. However Jane was under the influence of morphia, used to treat her depressive illness. She wrote the following in a letter to her husband, Thomas Carlyle (Jane was well known for her close attention to grammar):

".... it was settled that we should go yesterday to see St Mary's Loch and the Grey-Mares Tail - we started at nine of the morning in an open carriage. It was the loveliest of days and beautifuler scenery I never beheld; besides that it was full of tender interest for me, as the birth place of my mother - no pursuit of the Picturesque had ever gone better with me till, on the way back when we stopt to take a nearer inspection of the Tail - The Boys had been left fishing in the loch of the Lows. I quite forgot how old I was how out of the practice of "speeling rocks," and quite forgot too that John had made me take the night before a double dose of morphia which was still in my head making it very light - and I began to climb up the precipice!! - for a little way I got on well enough but when I discovered that I was climbing up a ridge (!) - that the precipice was not only behind but on both sides of me - I grew, for the first time in my life that I remember of, frightened - physically frightened - I was not only afraid of falling down - but of losing my head to the extent of throwing myself down - to go back on my hands and knees as I had come up was impossible - my only chance was to look at the grass under my face and toil on till John should see me. In my life I was never so thankful as when I found myself at the bottom of that hill with a glass of water to drink. It is a lovely place this - and a charming old-fashioned house *(Moffat House)* with "grounds" to the back. It is comfortably but plainly and old-fashionedly furnished - looks as if it had been stript of all its ornamental details - and just the necessaries left. There is a cook housemaid and ladysmaid and everything goes on very nicely." [211]

NOTES FOR TRAVELLERS.

BEATTOCK STATION is 61¼ miles per rail from Edinburgh, 64⅞ from Glasgow, and 39⅞ from Carlisle.

MOFFAT is nearly two miles from Beattock Station.

Trains leave Beattock Station (Caledonian Railway)

    For Edinburgh, at 6.56, 8.39, 10.24, a.m. ; 5.4, 6.43, and 8.15, p.m.

    For Glasgow at the same hours.

    For Carlisle, at 9.56, 11.12, a.m.; 4.1, 6.22, 8.21, and 10.40, p.m.

Omnibuses run to meet these trains from the "Annandale Arms Inn" (Mrs. Cranstoun's), in general about half an hour before railway time.

A Coach for Dumfries starts from the "Annandale Arms Inn" at 9.15, a.m.. and 7.45, p.m.

Conveyances of every description may be hired at Mrs. Cranstoun's, "Annandale Arms Inn," two doors north of the Office of this Paper.

Baths may be had (mineral, hot, cold, and shower,) at all hours of the day, in the Bath-room, to which an excellent Reading-room, Billiard-room, & Bowling-green are attached.

The Well is open every day from morning till night, and on Sabbath from 7 to 9, a.m., and from 5 to 7, p.m.

POST-OFFICE.—Despatches for Letters: London and South, 4.30, 9.15, p.m.; Edinburgh, Glasgow, and North: 6.45, 10.0, p.m.

The Postal Delivery begins at 8.15, a.m., and 7.15, p.m. Miss Grieve, postmistress, will give every information to commercial travellers and visitors on inquiry at the Office, Well Street.

The Moffat Register 1857 [212]

Visitor Numbers and House Building

On a single day in August of each year from 1866 to 1878 a census of visitors staying in Moffat was carried out. The average number during this period was 1,484 and the highest number was 2,149, in 1878. In 1874 there were 1,539 visitors of whom 359 were gentlemen, 681 ladies, 247 children, and 252 servants. In the early 1870s Moffat's three main hotels were full in the season. On a typical night in July 1872 there were 40 residents at the Annandale, 31 at the Buccleuch, and 21 at the Star.

By the 1870s there was sufficient accommodation in the town for about 2,200 visitors. In 1872, out of about 500 houses in the parish, over 200 offered lodging. This demand had helped to fuel a building boom in Moffat and the dwelling stock of the parish increased by 50% between 1851 and 1901, most of these built before 1881.

The grander villas constructed in Moffat during the late 18th Century and the earlier part of the 19th Century were generally built for the personal use of wealthy individuals. Burnbraes House (now the Well Road Centre) was built for Alexander Craig, a Moffat merchant; Amos House (now Dowding House) for James Amos who had made his money in the West Indies; Larchhill (1807) for Alexander Stevens, a wealthy Edinburgh man; Langshaw House for Major Johnstone, a retired military officer; and Sidmount (1832) for a retired Indian Army officer. Dumcrieff House (1823-1828) was rebuilt for Dr. John Rogerson on the proceeds of his work at the court of Catherine the Great of Russia.

In contrast, much of the new building in the third quarter of the 19th Century was speculative and designed mainly to reap profits from the demand for lodging houses in the town. For example the land now occupied by Hartfell Crescent was owned by Dr. Burnie of Bradford who planned the construction of 23 villas. The villas along the Ballplay and in Queensberry Terrace were built almost as a single development while those along Well Road were an early example of ribbon development. The houses in Beechgrove between the Academy and "the old suburban hamlet" of Havannah were built during the 1870s. Clarefoot and Vicarlands were completed in 1859, Hartfell Crescent in 1870, Queensberry Terrace, Dunmore Villa, Fairfield, Myrtle Bank, Viewfield, Greenwood Hall, and Charlie's Hope all in 1872.

Rooms, or entire houses, were offered for let at places such as Birnock Lodge, Union Villa, Glassmount Villa (now Hunter's Croft), Huntly Lodge, Shortwoodend, Burnbraes House, Park House, Elmhill, Roseville Cottage, Lyne Bank, Nethermill House, Clarefoot, Laurel Bank, Eden Cottage, Hartfell House, Corsleyburn, and Lime Tree House (St. Olaf).

Some Visitors Staying in Moffat on 19ᵗʰ September 1857

REGISTER.

LODGINGS.	VISITORS.	WHENCE.
Birnick Lodge—		
Mrs. J. L. Brown—	Mrs. Dalzell; Mrs. Miss & Capt. Baird;	
	Miss Carpandale,	Dumfries.
Union Villa—Mrs. Clark,	Mr. and Mrs. Gilmour and Family,	Glasgow.
	Mr. and Miss Pullan.	
Barnerook Villa—		
Mrs. Brydon—	Rev. Mr. and Miss Fairbairn,	Newhaven.
Roseburn Villa—		
Mrs. Fairbairn—	Rev. Dr. & Mrs. Tweedie and Family,	Edinburgh.
Glassmount Villa—		
Mrs. Beatson—	Mr. Sandeman and Family,	Glasgow.
Rosemount—		
Mrs. Turner—	Mrs. Miss and Mr. George Graham;	
	Miss Mill,	Shaw.
Green Bank—		
Mr. Tait—	Mrs. Miss and Captain Craigie,	
	Mrs. Miss and Mr. W. Lockhart.	
Millbank Place—		
Mrs. Dinwoodie—	Mrs. Fraser and Family,	Edinburgh.
Burnside Cottage—		
Mrs. Wilson—	Mrs. and Miss M'Bean,	Glasgow.
Burnbraes—		
Miss Macqueen—	Alexander Boggie, Esq.,	Liverpool.
Miss Syme—	Mr. and Mrs. Bogie and Family, Torquay, So. Devon.	
	Mr. M'Innes and Son.	Glasgow.
Mr. Dickson, Dyemill,	Mrs. Clementina, & Wm. Maxwell,	Terraughtie.
	Mr. Gunion and Family,	Edinburgh.
	Mr. R. and Miss Paul,	Dumfries.
	Rev. Mr. and Mrs. Alston.	
Meadow Cottages—		
Mrs. Tait—	R. Gilchrist, Esq., and Mrs. W. Gilchrist and Family,	Bothwell.
Mrs. John Bell—	Dr. and Mrs. Fairbairn,	Edinburgh.
Miss Beattie—	Mrs. Allan; Miss and W. G. Cassels,	Blackford Ho.,
		Edinburgh.
	Mrs. Willoughby; Miss M. Scott, St. Bernard's cresct.,	
		Edinburgh.
Miss Brown—	Mr. and Mrs. Wm. Liddel & Family,	Glasgow.
Miss Thomson—	Mrs. and Miss Grieve,	
Mrs. Martin—	Mr. Macadam,	Glasgow.
	Mr. Mrs. and Miss Fell.	
	Miss Swinebourne.	
	Mrs. and Miss Scott,	
Mrs. March—	Miss, and Miss J. M. Marshall,	Norham.
	Miss Cameron,	Edinburgh.
Miss Williamson—	Mrs. & Misses Fraser,	
	Mr. and Miss Drybrough, Windsor Villa, Edinburgh.	
	Miss Ogilvie,	Edinburgh.
Miss Hamilton—	Mr. and Mrs. Joseph Brown,	Edinburgh.
Burnhouse—		
Miss Johnstone—	Mr. and Mrs. Mitchel, Craigleith ho., Edinburgh.	
	Miss Gould, Beaconsfield Rectory, Buckinghamshire.	
	Mr. Gibson; Miss Brown,	Carlisle.
Mrs. Aitcheson—	Mrs. and Misses Anderson,	Edinburgh.
Miss Aitcheson—	Miss Laidlaw and Miss Russell,	Edinburgh.
Mrs. Hastie—	Rev. Mr. and Mrs. Philips,	Portobello.
Mrs. Murray—	Rev. Mr. and Mrs. Vary,	Pittenain.
Mrs. Kerr—	Mrs. and Miss Vary,	Crossford.
	Miss Craick,	St. Petersburg.
Mrs. Geo. Grieve—	Mrs. and Misses Osborne,	Workington.
	Mrs. Tripling,	Glasgow.
	Miss Campbell,	Portobello.
	Mrs. Alexander,	Glasgow.
Miss Grieve—	Captain and Mrs. M'Alpin & Family,	Greenock.
	Miss Cunningham and Miss Duncan,	Rothesay.
Mrs. Easton—	Mrs. Allister.	
Mrs. J. Johnstone—	Mrs. and Dr. Buchanan, H.E.I.C.S.,	Edinburgh.
	Captain N. L. Leslie,	London.
	Mrs. Carrick,	Edinburgh.
	Mrs. Allan,	Manchester.
	Messrs. Weardon,	Glasgow.
	Miss Wilson.	
Mrs. Crosbie—	Miss Sandeman,	Glasgow.
Miss Wilson—	Mr. Mrs. and Miss Lees.	
Mrs. Russell—	Mr. and Mrs. Cunningham,	Ormiston.

LODGINGS.	VISITORS.	WHENCE.
Miss Wightman—	Mr. Aikman,	Glasgow.
	Miss Ferguson, Misses More,	Edinburgh.
	Master James and Charles More,	Edinburgh.
Mrs. Thos. Henderson—	Mr. and Mrs. Frazer,	Glasgow.
Mr. H. Wilson—	Misses Birrell.	
Mrs. Watt—	Mrs. and Miss Robertson.	
Mrs. Scott—	Miss Currie.	
	Mr. and Mrs. Rawdon and Son,	York.
Miss Wilson—	Rev. J. H. Howson,	Dirleton.
	Rev. D. K. Dowie,	Large.
	Misses Leslie,	Markinch.
Miss Jardine—	Miss Bell; Miss Simpson; Miss Mordoff; Miss Mordy,	Workington.
Mrs. J. L. Brown—	Mrs. Greaves and Family.	
Mrs. Tait—	Mrs. Binnie and Family,	Glasgow.
Mrs. Archd. Morison—	Adam Smith, Esq., and Family,	Dunbreck.
Mrs. Dr. Dalgleish—	Mr. and Mrs. Laing,	Glasgow.
	Mr. & Mrs. Park and Son, Abbot's Meadow, Melrose.	
	Mr. and Mrs. Gordon,	Workington.
	Miss Macpherson,	Edinburgh.
Mrs. Henderson—	Miss Whitehead,	Paisley.
	Miss Spreull,	Glasgow.
Miss Gibson—	Misses Carson,	Edinburgh.
	Mr. and Mrs. Drummond,	Edinburgh.
	Miss Johnstone,	Cowhill. Dumfries.
Miss Hunter—	Mr. Milligan,	Rio Janeiro.
	Miss Ashbridge—	Hendingham.
Mrs Carruthers—	Mr. More; Mrs. Wood; Miss Richardson, Whitehaven.	
Mrs. James Kerr—	Mr. and Mrs. R. B. Handyside,	Glasgow.
	Miss Handyside,	Glasgow.
Mrs. Stewart—	Major and Miss Gordon,	Edinburgh.
Mr. Nelson—	Mrs. and Misses Maxwell,	Edinburgh.
Roseville Cottage—		
Mrs. Marjoribank—	Mr. Thomson; Miss Fenwick.	
Miss Harkness—	Thomas Watson, Esq.,	Glasgow.
	J. T. Dickie, Esq.,	Glasgow.
	Dr. and Mrs. Martin and Family,	Edinburgh.
Mrs. Alex. Morrison—	Dr. and Miss Mitchell and Son.	
Mrs. S. Cowan—	Mr. Murdoch,	Glasgow.
Mrs. Wm. Halliday—	Mr. and Mrs. Gibson,	St. Andrews.
Miss A. Halliday—	Mr. and Miss Ostell and Miss Barns,	Glasgow.
Mrs. John Edgar—	Mr. Moir.	
Mrs. Dr. Scott—	Mr. and Mrs. Longcake,	Alloa.
Mrs. Rogerson—	Rev. Mr. Bremner,	Gorbals, Glasgow.
Mrs. D. Johnstone—	Captain Campbell,	Whitehaven.
Mrs. Renwick—	Misses Hind,	Whitehaven.
Mrs. Watson—	Mrs. Heath,	London.
Miss Owen—	Mr. and Mrs. Ogilvie and Family,	London.
Elmhill—Mrs. Hamilton,	Mr. and Mrs. Thomson,	Eaglesham.
Mr. Sinclair—	Mrs. and Miss R. Fairbairn,	Leeds. Yorkshire.
	Miss Rathbone and Miss Vaucher,	Liverpool.
	Miss Forster,	Carlisle.
Mrs. Stevenson—	Mrs. Lyall and Son; Miss Galloway;	
	Mrs. Morrison,	Glasgow.
Miss Clapperton—	Mr. and Mrs. Roxburgh,	Airus.
Mrs. Martin—	Mrs. and Mr. J. Cochrane,	Glasgow.
Mrs. Richardson—	Mrs. and Miss M'Donald,	Glasgow.
Mrs. Murray—	Mr. and Mrs. Wilson and Family,	Cambusiang.
Victoria Place—		
Mrs. Johnstone—	Hugh Handyside, Esq.,	Edinburgh.
Miss Kirkpatrick—	Mr. Mrs. and Mr. Thos. Dowie,	Leith.
	Mrs. and Miss Ritchie,	Stansfield.
	Mr. and Mrs. W. A. Ritchie,	Bombay C.S.
	Mrs. Bellard,	Liverpool.
Mrs. Henry—	Mr. and Mrs. Page and Family,	St. Albans.
Mrs. Rankine—	Mr. and Miss Pears,	Edinburgh.
Mrs. Barbour—	Mr. and Mrs. Steele,	Glasgow.
Mrs. Earsman—	Mrs. and Miss Clementson.	
Spur Cottage—		
Mrs. P. Halliday—	Mr. Mrs. and Misses Wilson.	
	Mrs. Ferron,	Crosby.
Mrs. Earsman—	Mr. & Mrs. Stirling; Mr. A. Stirling, Musselburgh.	
Mrs. Gilland—	Mr. and Mrs. Hills and Family,	Glasgow.
Beechgrove—		
Mrs. Ewart—	Mr. and Mrs. M'Geoch and Family,	Glasgow.
Mrs. Proudfoot—	Mr. and Miss Sheriffs,	Aberdeen.

Printed and Published by Wm. Murs, Bookseller and Stationer, High Street, Moffat.

REGISTER OF FURNISHED HOUSES AND LODGINGS.

(WILLIAM MUIR & Co., Booksellers, High Street, keep a Register of all the Houses and Lodgings in Moffat and Neighbourhood, and application to them, personally or by letter, will receive immediate attention.)

A common let is for two months; June and July going together, and August and September. This arrangement is always studied in respect of houses which let self-contained; but of course it is not always practicable. In large houses, where attendance is given, the let may be in whole, or in apartments, as the parties see right to arrange. Attendance is the general rule; and, in such cases, no mark of reference is given in the following list. Houses with the mark * let either self-contained or with attendance. The mark † denotes that the house lets self-contained only. The letters "S" and "C" mean stable and coach-house on the premises.

HIGH STREET, West Side, South to North.

Mrs Crosbie—parlour and 2 bed-rooms (1 double).
Mrs Brown—1 sitting, 2 bed-rooms, and attic.
Mrs S. Carruthers—1 sitting, 3 bed-rooms, and 2 attics.
Mrs H. Wilson—2 parlours and 3 bed-rooms.
Mrs Moffat—parlour and 2 bed-rooms.
Mrs Sanders—2 sitting, 3 bed-rooms, and 3 attics.
Mr W. Muir—parlour and 2 bed-rooms.
Mrs Somerville—parlour and 3 bed-rooms.
Miss Murray (No. 20)—3 sitting and 8 bed-rooms (2 double).
Mrs Harland—parlour and bed-room.

BANK SQUARE.
Or South Side of High Street, West to East.

Mrs Marshall—2 parlours and 6 bed-rooms.
Mrs Scott—parlour, 3 bed-rooms (1 double).

HIGH STREET, East Side, South to North.

Miss Currie—2 sitting, 8 bed-rooms (2 double).
Proudfoot Place—Mrs Dalglish—3 sitting and 8 bed-rooms.
Bath Place. { Mrs Little—parlour and 4 bed-rooms.
Miss Douglas—2 parlours, 5 bed-rooms, and 2 attics.
Mrs Young—parlour and 3 bed-rooms.
Mrs T. Hetherington—2 sitting and 5 bed-rooms (1 double).

Well, The.

Terms for Visiting Moffat Mineral Well and drinking the Water: Ladies and Gentlemen, 6d per week each, paid in advance; less than a week, 2d per day. A Family, including children, 2s 6d per week. Trades' People of Moffat, Servants, and Labourers, half these rates. A Quart or Bottle of Water at the Well, ½d; Delivered at the Visitor's Lodgings, 1d. Well Keeper—Mrs Linton, Well Cottage. Well Water Carrier—Ann Richardson, Burgess's Close, off High Street.

Moffat Directory and Visitors' Guide for 1874. William Muir and Co. (1874)

1854 Thomas Carlyle was finding the pace of change in Moffat almost too much to bear, but he is not specific about the causes of his discontent:

> "Alas, Moffat is a changed place to you; a sadly changed place even to me when I think of it! But we must not look too much behind; we must do what is at hand and ahead; our life, and what we have to do, is still ahead." [213]

1854 William Keddie, now Professor William Keddie, provided an account of the growing strengths of Moffat as a travel destination:

> "Moffat is becoming the summer resort of our Glasgow citizens, who are succeeded in autumn by equal number of the citizens of Edinburgh, and while these seek its bracing air, its trouting streams, and varied and inviting walks, for the purposes of healthful relaxation from business, medical men are more than ever sending dyspeptic and other patients to drink its waters and inhale its fresh breezes, away from the turmoil of business and the constrained and artificial habits of the great city." [214]

1854 In March, Britain and France had declared war on Russia and the Crimean War began. Feelings were running high at this time and in October a bonfire was built outside Moffat House. A figure of Tsar Nicholas I (the same Nicholas who had visited Moffat in 1817), elegantly and tastefully dressed, had been carefully crafted by a number of young ladies belonging to the party of the Hon. Leslie-Melville who was staying at Moffat House. The Tsar was pelted and shot at by fireworks of all kinds before the bonfire was lit. As the flames curled round the imperial figure, three groans for Nicholas were called for and given with much energy and expression. The Russian flag was then burned and two volleys of shot were then fired as a finale to the evening. [215]

1857 In May the weather in Edinburgh was particularly cold and this angler was reviewing the prospects of finding some sport:

> " It is now very near the middle of May ... and yet there is no burst of verdure on the trees ..... An obdurate, cold, dry east wind has the monopoly of the compass, reddening the

noses, ruffling the skins, irritating the throats, and destroying the tempers of het Majesty's liege subjects of Edinburgh ... Where are they to fly to? Moffat, if the account of two shivering explorers can be believed, is still as cheerless as Spitzbergen." [216]

1857 In the summer Dr. Norman Macleod stayed at Craigieburn House with his mother, wife, and children. Whilst at Craigieburn he meditated and wrote "The Gold Thread". On July 7th, Dr. Macleod wrote a letter from Craigieburn to one of his associates:

"Here I am, like a blackbird reposing in my nest in a green wood, beside a burn, surrounded by pastoral hills, musical with bleating sheep and shadowy with clouds. My chicks all about me, some chirping, some singing, all gaping for food, with my lady blackbird perched beside me, her glossy plumage glittering in the sun, a perfect sermon on contentment.

Blackbirds put me in mind of bills, and bills of money, and money of those who need it, and then of those who are willing to give it, and that brings me to you. It is not for schools, churches or schemes, but for charity, to help a needy gentlewoman.....

I am sorry to say that my complaint has not left me. I had a learned consultation in London with the great authority in such cases. He has put me on a regimen so strict that it would make a hermit's cell almost comfortable ; and he commands rest. But this I cannot command for a month yet." [217]

On an evening in August, before he left his summer quarters, Dr. Macleod bade farewell to the people of Moffatdale by preaching on a green knowe at Craigieburn. Almost 800 people were there to hear him. [218]

1857 In September, William Keddie was again promoting the attractions of Moffat in an article in the *Scottish Guardian*:

"This far-famed and long-established watering place, so cheering from the surpassing beauty of the surrounding scenery, so invigorating from the salubrity of its atmosphere, and felt to be so beneficial from the healthful virtue of the mineral spring, has since about the middle of July been a central focus of attraction. It has been visited by a vast concourse of the different ranks and professions, including the sons and daughters of opulence, from almost every corner of the kingdom and adjoining borders, who have repaired to this lovely and inviting vale. During one week the number of visitors considerably exceeded what it had hitherto been wont to do since the discovery of the medicinal well; for during that week it was estimated there were not less than 900 to 1,000 persons .... Nor has anything been awanting on the part of the more influential inhabitants of Moffat to augment the felicity of the various visitors who have repaired from afar to witness its picturesque rural scenes and glens, which unfold the richest fields for botanical research and disquisition. An instrumental band was early in the season engaged for the entertainment of the gay and noble, as well as innocent relaxation of the learned who might come amongst them for the summer and autumnal seasons." [219]

Garpol Glen and Beld Craig [220]

1858 In August, an unnamed visitor who was kindly disposed to Moffat wrote to the *Moffat Register* to suggest some improvements:

"... a fund should be raised for the purpose of laying out certain of the walks around Moffat for pleasure promenades. The walk along the Annan bank should be smoothed, laid, seated etc. and a rustic bridge should be thrown over about midway between the two existing stone bridges, and that the other side of the river be also made able to be walked upon. The road to the Gallow-hill should be as much improved as possible by the cutting out of stumps, roots etc., and the softening of the pathway to the foot. The road across Coates Hill is also susceptible of great improvement, especially in its earlier part, which is anything but inviting.

These suggestions would be thorough and appreciable improvements, which visitors would enjoy and inhabitants themselves would relish ... they might be most advantageously extended to the cutting of a traverse-able-for-ladies road way to the hollow basin into which the Grey Mare's Tail is precipitated.

Our fine, broad, open street, so well lined with elegant houses and excellent shops, is a most agreeable and pleasant promenade; but some may wish to be away from the public gaze, to be in retirement, to hear the murmur of the gently flowing waters rather than the hum of trade, and the rustle of the leaves than the roll of vehicles." [221]

1858 Robert Blakey was back again and he stayed at an inn at Tweedshaws where he had a thoroughly good time:

"After several hours of hard riding we arrived at the little inn at Tweedshaws, and found it almost choke full of tourists like ourselves; but we failed to recognize among the company any of our friends from the west. In the course, however, of a few hours we had the pleasure of seeing and shaking them cordially by the hand. The party consisted of a Dr. Reid, from Carlisle, and two Italian noblemen, who had sought refuge in this country from the political troubles and devastations of their own, occasioned by the revolutionary army of France. The inn we then occupied stood at that time on the opposite side of the ravine from the one which now goes by the name of Tweedshaws. It was a very small place, with a low and thatched roof, and only contained two principal apartments, in addition to two or three nooks or boxes in the attic to serve for bed-rooms.

After regaling ourselves with some fine bacon-collops and eggs, and good ale (for the main stock of the vender had been sent by a servant in a dog-cart to the Crook Inn, about ten miles further down the Tweed), we commenced looking about our fishing gear, but previously resolved, ere we began angling operations, to take a short saunter to the west of the inn, to view what is called the "Devil's Beef-tub". This is a steep mountain, about fifteen hundred feet high, which forms at its base a large well-rounded circular space like a cauldron or tub: hence its name. It is unquestionably a great natural curiosity, and we believe it is now much frequented by tourists who journey through this part of Scotland. On our return to the thatched inn, we resolved to have a little angling." [222]

1858   An article in the *Whitehaven Herald* was critical of the lack of accommodation in Moffat:

"The omnibuses come up from Beattock, crowded to overflowing, four times a day. Many persons so arriving can find no place to occupy, and return by rail to other quarters. Of these places I find the Bridge of Allan the most attractive. Late the other night a gentleman begged so piteously to be allowed even to sleep in the garret, that our landlord and his missus – kind hearts! – granted the request; and, as expected, in the morning the gentleman moved off to the Bridge of Allan. We, in the lower rooms, found the heat oppressive; what must he have experienced under the heated slates?" [223]

1859   In May, a long article about Moffat appeared in the *Dumfries Courier*. The length and tone of the full article suggests that it was a bad week for newspaper stories in Dumfries. This extract gives us the flavour:

"The weather in Moffat is more than charming – delicious. The extreme bright blueness of the sky is softened by the festooned drapery of cloud that forms a canopy for the regal sun to dwell in. The mystic life of the atmosphere is enriched by the pleasing incense of the blooming earth, the quiver of foliage, rich, ripe, and sight-refreshing in its greenness; as well as the many-melodied songs of the gladsome birds. Its *(Moffat's)* fine southern exposure gives it an exquisitely facile enjoyment of the "nectarous gold" of the sunshine; while its nook-shotten quietness at the foot of the fine range of hills supplies it with fresh mountain breezes, and gives a visitor the choice of roaming in the shadowy passes of the hill country, or wandering in the cheerful loveliness of the plain." [224]

1859 Not to be outdone, the *Dumfries Herald* followed up in the next week with an equally elaborate description of the town:

"We are now verging upon our "Season"; our streets are already flooded with sunlight, and they will shortly be floating with muslin. The arsenals of trade will empty their worn-hearted and anxious-brained from the railway carriages into our nature-gifted locality; and the severer duties of necessity will for a time be replaced by rewarding, re-invigorating, and renewing relaxation. The toil and moil of tense thought will be exchanged for rest and enjoyment; and the ledger will be closed for a while, that the heart may rejoice in the ledger-demain of beauty." [225]

1859 In September, a positively effusive account of Moffat appeared in the *Dunfermline Journal*:

"A moral beauty crowns the scene *(of Moffat and Upper Annandale)* .... realising even in the midst of our utilitarian age - and within sound of the railway whistle too - the pastoral simplicity and Arcadian peace of the olden time, as sung by the poets.

The houses *(of Moffat)* are built of the greywacke rock of the district, a tough and compact stone of a bluish colour, well fitted for the purpose, and when faced with white sandstone, and when not blackened by an artificial process sometimes resorted to, they have a light and agreeable appearance, especially when ornamented in front with climbing rose-bushes or trellised flowers.

With the exception of the villas on the road to the Well, some of which are elegant and fashionable edifices, the general aspect of the place may be described as plain and neat, rather than showy. One feature which strikes every visitor is the exceeding cleanliness of the houses and streets, and the tidy habits of the people ... Moffat is exempt from any known distemper, and from the epidemic fevers which afflict our large towns; it even escaped the cholera when it was decimating the inhabitants of Dumfries.

In noticing the cleanly habits of the people, it is also due to them to state that they are equally remarkable for their civility and attention to strangers. Indeed the peasantry of the district have long been noted for their intelligence and native courtesy, in which qualities the villagers largely share; and one sees amongst them none of that tendency to exaction, not to say unscrupulousness and greed, which but too commonly characterise people elsewhere who have been more accustomed to depend upon an annual influx of visitors.

The Lord's day is observed with great decorum, a good sign of a village, as well as of a family or an individual." [226]

1859 An unnamed visitor wrote about Moffat Well. One wonders which music would be appropriate to accompany the drinking of water:

"On a fine morning the walk is very picturesque and enjoyable and the Band of Music is stationed at the Well to assist the drinking - three large tumblers being the statutory quantum. As several hundred usually assemble at this time, the Well is not a little gay and the walk there and back does much to appetise the visitors for breakfast - the lazy, infirm or juvenile having, however, the facility of riding in a bus." [227]

Announcement in *The Scotsman* 1859 [228]

1860 "Wanderer" wrote in New Sporting Magazine:

"...we reached Moffat and were rattled up to the Annandale Arms - an excellent and capacious house, replete with every comfort and convenience, including a billiard table, together with civility and good attendance .... we wended our way to Moffat Spa, distant a mile and a half from the village, and whither numbers were proceeding in order to drink the water ... On reaching the well-known house, a strong odour announced the presence of the sulphureous water, of which several of both sexes were partaking, the countenances of two or three ladies being highly expressive of a certain amount of nausea at the draught. In defiance of this we drank of a good-sized tumbler, and, although certainly not to be called delicious, we found it by no means so unpalatable as we expected, nor was this the only trial of it during our sojourn at Moffat. The charge made for this water is twopence for the first glass, after which a person is permitted to drink it *ad libitum* during the Saturday; or sixpence a week; one shilling and threepence for a family of three persons; one shilling and sixpence for a family of four; for the tradespeople of Moffat a halfpenny per day; for the water when carried away, threepence per dozen bottles; while a penny per bottle is charged for it when brought into the village.

Moffat ... , difficult of access in coaching days, has been placed within the reach of persons from all parts of the kingdom, both as regards their time and pockets .... the Baths, adjoining the Annandale Arms Hotel, the charges are, vapour 2s., warm mineral 2s., warm common 1s., cold shower 6d., tepid shower 1s." [229]

1860 The Moffat area is botanically rich and in the 19th Century over half of the species of ferns found in the United Kingdom could be found in the vicinity. Changes in agricultural practices, and the Victorian passion for plant collecting, had a significant impact upon the local flora. Two publications from the 1860s provided detailed information on local ferns, detailed descriptions of where to find them, and pages to fill with pressed specimens. [230] [231] In October 1860, John Sadler, a notable botanist of the time, wrote to the *Moffat Register* from the Royal Botanic Garden in Edinburgh. John provided some mixed messages about the desirability of plant-hunting:

"Having occasion to spend a few hours in your delightful neighbourhood last week, I paid a hasty visit to "Woodsia Ravine", to see how my dear pet of a fern was prospering in its mountain solitude. After passing the 7th milestone from Moffat I entered Woodsia Ravine, properly speaking Correifron Burn. On reaching the far end of the Correi, I searched for a considerable time before I discovered any specimen of the little fern, - high up beyond my reach, and not likely ever to be disturbed by human hands. In my endeavour, however, to obtain it, I regret to say that I nearly lost my life, and got a tremendous fright, for my foot slipped on the verge of a savage precipice, and left me suspended for a moment or two over the thundering flood far beneath.

Although I did not obtain the plant, yet I almost wish every other specimen was in a like position. It was with feelings of disgust, if not rage, that I read the other day in a botanical publication – "A few days ago I gathered fourteen luxuriant plants of the rare *Woodsia ilvensis* in Moffatdale in less than an hour." This was from the pen of an English nurseryman who is now disposing of these plants to the public at half-a-guinea each. I am confident you will agree with me when I say surely such a sordid collector deserves every scientific botanist's anathema!

P.S. I wish you could stimulate some of the Moffatonians or of your many visitors to botanise a little about the neighbourhood, and to leave dried specimens of the plants with you, for the inspection of botanists. It is only by such united labours that we can ever hope to arrive at a correct knowledge of the Flora of the district." [232]

1861 The Hiring Fair was held on 29th March, which was Good Friday. The following report gives a good impression of the nature and scale of the event:

"The market is looked forward to with great expectations by the whole surrounding country along the Scottish borders and numbers its frequenters from the Tweed, the Yarrow, the Esk, the Nith, and the Dee, as well as the more adjacent parts of the south of Scotland.

By early morning the roads leading to Moffatwards were dotted with passengers in all sorts of gearing – on foot, in cart, on pony-back, and in gig or carriage. The morning trains brought loads to the omnibuses, and by 10.30 or so the usual stance at the "Mercat Cross" was thronged with folks in search of their "penny fee", and masters and mistresses on the look out for "guid" servants. Of course, hiring began at high rates ... ; young ploughmen were hired at from £9 to £10; woman servants, indoor, from £2 10s. to £3 10s.; outdoor from £4 10s. to £5 5s. General farm servants were greatly in demand, and very few were left unhired.

In the hope of mitigating the evils - especially of drunkenness - too frequent at hiring fairs, several influential gentlemen had arranged to use some combined efforts. One of these was the opening of our large bath's assembly-hall for the vendication of tea, coffee, and their accompaniments, at a moderate cost. During the early part of the day - though we did not observe much diminution in the drink traffic - no instance of disorderliness occurred." [233]

1861 An unnamed writer warned of the dangers of binge-drinking:

"In Scotland we have but few watering-places, and none of remarkable efficacy. Strathpeffer, Moffat, and the Bridge of

Allan are nevertheless much resorted to, and in their respective seasons, crowds repair to the wells and guzzle water without stint or measure. No discretion is observed by those daring deglutators of the element. The prevalent notion seems to be that the more tumblers a man can swallow, the speedier will be his cure; and, to judge from the quantity consumed, one would naturally suppose that the patients were afflicted with an unappeasable hereditary thirst. No symptoms of hydrophobia there, but a vigorous contention for the pitcher. Now this is a vast mistake. All kinds of mineral water should be used cautiously and in moderation, and never without medical assurance that they are strictly suitable for the removal of the complaint." [234]

1861 At the end of October, the Hon. The Earl of Leven and Melville, Lady Leven, and Viscount Kirkcaldy who had their summer and autumn quarters at Moffat House, left Moffat *en route* for his Lordship's mansion at Roehampton in Surrey. Before leaving, his Lordship entertained the children attending the various schools in Moffat to tea, romping on the lawn etc. The ascent of London-bought balloons caused much excitement. [235]

HYDROPATHIC ESTABLISHMENT.
MOFFAT.
JAMES FERGUSSON, M.D., respectfully intimates that he has OPENED a HYDROPATHIC ESTABLISHMENT at VICARLAND PARK, one of the Suburban Villas of this Favourite and Fashionable Watering-Place.
Prospectuses forwarded on application to himself, or Mr Wm. Muir, Bookseller, Moffat.
Moffat, 4th June 1863   87

Announcement in *The Scotsman* 1864 [236]

1863 In 1853 it had been reported that some gold had been found in the past in Moffat Water and in other streams in Upper Annandale. Perhaps in response to this report, the following appeared in 1859:

"Mr. Griffin, a gentleman from Leamington, has this week passed through Moffat provided with all tools necessary for gold digging and washing, accompanied by two miners from Leadhills. The scenes of their explorations are to be the head of Moffat side and in the neighbourhood of St. Mary's Loch." [237]

There is no record of Mr. Griffin's success in his mission. However small finds of gold were made near Megget Water in 1863 and a small nugget, weighing about 6 grains, was shown to many in Moffat. [238]

1864 In July a correspondent to the *Caledonian Mercury* had some good words to say about the "Star":

"There are three good hotels in Moffat in any one of which the tourist can have every comfort. One of them – the "Star", Mr. J.L. Brown – has adopted the custom now universally followed in the best hotels in Harrogate, of a fixed tariff per day, to include board, lodging and service. The figure at the Star is 5s.6d. per day.

People however who intend to stay for any length of time usually prefer to take private lodgings, and everything of this kind, from an entire villa, completely furnished, down or rather up to a garret, can be had to suit the means and tastes of visitors. We have observed this year that houses with lawns in front of them are most in request, the game of croquet, which is at present so popular with the rising generation, requiring a green sward." [239]

M O F F A T S P A
THE STAR HOTEL.

For the convenience and advantage of temporary Visitors to MOFFAT, the Proprietor of the STAR HOTEL has made arrangements for the introduction of a New System of Charges on the Model of the English Hotels at Harrogate and other Watering Places – viz. (1or Terms to be moderate and fixed, the Cuisine of best quality, Wine and Spirits to be charged extra.

Terms, including Board, Lodging, and Service per Day.
: in Public,........................... 6s. 6d.
" including Board, Lodging, and Service
in Private,........................... 7s. 6d.
" Servants' Board and Lodging,........... 5s. 0d.
Beds charged extra if only for Two Nights.
Private Sitting-Rooms 2s per Day, and 1s. for Service for each Person. Horses at Hay 10s. 6d. per Week, Ostler and Boots extra. A Lock-up Coach-House.
Commercial Gentlemen will find this Hotel equally moderate in charges, and everything served up of fine quality.
Soups, Chops, and Steaks on short notice; Suppers, &c. The Hotel is convenient and suitable in the Town, being only two minutes from the Public Baths, Bowling-Green, and Billiard Room. From the Windows is a fine prospect of the surrounding scenery, limited only by distant hills.
Beattock Station for Moffat, on Caledonian Railway, is 1¾ miles from Carlisle, 60 from Edinburgh and Glasgow. Two 'Buses attend the Trains, either of which will take up or put down passengers at the Star Hotel when requested to do so.
Intending Visitors to Moffat can have information about Lodgings in Town by inclosing a directed stamp envelope.
6474   JAMES L. BROWN, Proprietor.

Announcement in *The Scotsman* 1864 [240]

Disease and Life Expectancy

In the late 1850s, the average male Scot had a 1 in 7 chance of dying before his first birthday and a life expectancy of 40. Today, he has a 1 in 200 chance of dying before his first birthday and a life expectancy of 74 (79 for females).

In Moffat, of the 51 children born between 1855 and 1865 with the surname Johnstone, 15 (30%) had died before the age of 16. Of these, 5 died from postnatal complications, 3 from scarlet fever, 3 from diarrhoea (possibly a complication of scarlet fever), 1 from diphtheria, 1 from typhoid fever, and 2 from other causes. However, children in Moffat were safer than in most other places, particularly compared with urban areas. Infant mortality rates (deaths in the first year of life) were 95 per 1,000 live births in Dumfriesshire in 1861 compared to 147 per 1,000 in Lanarkshire and 131 in Lothian.

Smallpox was a leading cause of death until the 19th Century, the great majority of victims being young children. Almost everyone suffered at some time from the disease and one in every five deaths was directly, or indirectly, attributable to smallpox. About 30% of those infected died, including 80% of children under 5 years of age, and one third of the survivors became blind. It affected all social classes and many of the patients who recovered were disfigured. The disease was endemic in large cities but in small towns such as Moffat epidemics of the disease occurred in cycles of about 5 years.

Cholera is a water-borne disease typically contracted from drinking contaminated water. Dumfries was visited by a cholera epidemic in 1832, when 421 persons died, and again in 1848, when the disease claimed another 317. Moffat was entirely spared, largely due to the cleanliness of the local water supply.

Scarlet fever is a streptococcal infection which, if untreated, has some very dangerous complications. An epidemic in 1874-75 claimed 11,000 lives in Scotland.

Until the early 1950s, pulmonary tuberculosis was endemic and was still one of the greatest killers of young adults, particularly young women, just as diphtheria was the great killer of young children. As late as May 1901 there was a serious outbreak of diphtheria in the Evan Valley, apparently arising from serious sanitary defects at the local school. At least three cases were fatal and a temporary isolation hospital was erected at Middlegill. This hospital treated 29 cases of diphtheria before it was closed in September 1901.

In September, an anonymous visitor was sitting in the Buccleuch Arms when he wrote to the *Glasgow Herald*. His comments about the town's drainage system may have been prompted by the smell from Moffat's three open sewers, one of which ran along the west side of the High Street and in front of the Buccleuch Arms. If the weather was very dry then the sluggish flow in the sewers was relieved by digging out the raw sewage and piling it on the adjacent road. This had inevitable and unpleasant results in warm weather:

> "Here I am, at the comfortable hotel of my old friend Mrs. Cranstoun. It seems like a dream to look back on my youthful days spent here. Well do I remember Humphry Cranstoun, then occupying the Spur Inn, over forty summers ago. This house is most comfortable, and the servants civil and obliging. Any one who has a few days to spare cannot do better than take up their abode at Mrs. Cranstoun's. Ma conscience, what breakfasts! I have no wish to disparage the Annandale Arms and the Star, for I have it from good authority that they are well-conducted houses, and charges reasonable. While therefore there are good hotels and lodgings at Moffat, it has long been a reproach of the *natives* that this pretty little village is without drainage or a supply of pure water, with all their attendant conveniences and comforts. I am credibly informed there are over 1,000 strangers here at present, and while they are well supplied with butcher meats, bread, dairy produce etc., they are generally loud in their complaints of the lack of indoor conveniences, now so universal in all towns.
>
> After a supply of water and drainage has been accomplished, I hope the next move will be a meeting of the inhabitants of the village and neighbourhood, when a unanimous resolution will be passed to apply to the Home Secretary for an order to shut up the old burying-ground, so offensively kept in every respect, and so injurious to health.
>
> The village owns three branch banks – Union Bank of Scotland, Bank of Scotland, and British Linen – the latter a new and substantial, but rather sombre building. On the whole, I think Moffat is greatly improved since I was here three or four years ago; but while I am always disposed to

praise Moffat and neighbourhood, there is one thing I would call particular attention to, and I hope that those interested will at once see to the condition of the Academy and Burgh School. To attempt to describe the unsatisfactory state of the whole premises, the wanton destruction of the desks, forms, doors etc. etc. would not be easy; I will only add, "Go and judge for yourself"." [241]

A Thistle-Stop Tour

The editor of the *Moffat Register* provided this itinerary which appeared in *The Scotsman* of 9th June 1862:

"An enterprising tourist may quit "the grey metropolis of the North" *(Edinburgh)* on Saturday morning, flash by the North British Railway to Galashiels and thence by branch to Selkirk (39½ miles); take coach hence for St. Mary's, run through the plain of Philiphaugh, the Vale of Yarrow, pass Bowhill, Newark Castle, Fowlshiels, the birth-place of Mungo Park, Yarrow Church, Douglas Water, St. Mary's Kirk and, landing at "the hallowed mere" (19½ miles), dine. Then, taking the Moffat return omnibus, may skirt the "Watch Hill", see "the loftiest cascade in the Queen's Britannic dominions", and, following the example of its waters, drive down the pass of Moffat Dale (15 miles). Tea taken at Moffat, and 'bus to Beattock Station (2 miles) on the Caledonian line, and reach Edinburgh (61 miles) before the chimes of St. Gile's strike midnight, after an "out" of nearly 130 miles of matchless scenery dipped in the fairy tints of poesy by Scott, Hogg, Burns, Wordsworth, Mayne, the old balladists etc., and of greater variety than almost any route of the same length in any other country affords".

1865 Alexander Murray painted a very favourable view of the town. In doing so he constructed one of the longest sentences known in the literature of travel:

"As a town the situation of Moffat is excellent, and so healthy that, when Dumfries was scourged by the cholera visitation, none suffered in Moffat. The main street of the town is broad, the trade done considerable, and the villas which year by year, in increasing numbers, are rising in the neighbourhood, strengthen the estimation in which the place stands with the valetudinarian; accommodation in house or hotel being ample and excellent, the number of visitors great, society good, there being an assembly-room, reading-room, libraries, and many other modes of making the stay there a pleasant one for the stranger." [242]

MOFFAT–HOTEL REMOVAL

MRS CRANSTOUN—who for thirty-two years has conducted a HOTEL BUSINESS in MOFFAT, latterly at the house presently known as "THE ANNANDALE ARMS HOTEL"—begs to intimate that she will REMOVE to her own PREMISES, which she has extended, improved, and refitted, and which will be now known as

CRANSTOUN'S BUCCLEUCH ARMS HOTEL.

At the same time, she takes this opportunity of returning her thanks to the Nobility, Gentry, and Commercial Gentlemen generally, as well as the Inhabitants of and Visitors to Moffat, for their lengthened and much esteemed patronage –of which she hopes to merit a continuance.

Ample Stable accommodation, Omnibuses to the trains as usual, Conveyances of all kinds on hire.   3383

Announcement in *The Scotsman* 1863 [243]

1865 James Bertram bemoaned the impact of crowds of railborne anglers on the local fish stocks:

"... fish are not so plentiful as they were thirty years ago, in the old coaching days, when it was possible to fill a washing-tub in the space of half an hour with lovely half-pond trout from a few pools on a burn near Moffat." [244]

1866 An interesting description of the Baths Hall appeared:

"In front of this building, which was erected in 1827, with a Grecian portico, is a fine large room, occupied during the day as a reading room, at 1/- per week, or 6/- per quarter in advance, and serving also as a town-hall, as well as being used for public meetings, concerts, balls, soirees, school examinations etc. etc., and, during "the season", vocal or instrumental concerts every evening, at a charge of 6d. admission, with the exception of Friday, when there was a ball or promenade. A good instrumental band from Glasgow or Edinburgh is engaged every season for these concerts, and also to perform at the Well every morning. Attached to the Baths are a billiard-room and bowling-green; and at the bowling "tournaments", open to the whole country, prizes of considerable value are contended for." [245]

Announcement in *The Scotsman* 1865 [246]

1869 A letter appeared in the *Liverpool Mail* and it was quoted in full in the *Moffat Times* of 4th September 1869. The letter was signed by "A Visitor in 1868":

"Moffat Spa is proverbially the 'Harrogate of Scotland' and without the dignified aspect or the fashionable rackettings of Harrogate, or Buxton, of Leamington, or Cheltenham, or Bath. If you want a really efficacious village and almost mountain spa - and with the grandest scenery into the bargain - we say "Try Moffat Spa". Best of all, there is excellent and economical accommodation for all classes of visitors at Moffat, including several really moderate hotels, such as the Annandale Arms, the Star, the Buccleuch Arms, the Beattock Hotel, and smaller ones.

We have sojourned more than once in Moffat, and for a month together, and we know no watering-place in Scotland, England or Ireland, where you find more obliging tradesmen and shopkeepers ... As regards the scenery the excursions both longer and shorter are not to be excelled in all the southern half of Scotland." [247]

1869 A rather more jaundiced letter to the *Dumfries Herald* was again quoted in full in the *Moffat Times*:

"The charges at the hotels (in Moffat) are extremely moderate, and everything of the best quality. Lodgings are high, so much as £45 per month being given for months together for houses, the annual rent of which is only £50 or £60. Letting lodgings is a complete trade, and verily a very profitable one in Moffat. All the inhabitants seem bent on money-making .... and even children of the very smallest size go gathering and hawking for sale blueberries, mushrooms, and ferns, and bottles of water from the Well and different springs round Moffat, selling the same at goodly profit. Velocipedes are hired out by the hour - in short it is impossible to enumerate the devices in Moffat to make money.

It is strange what the facilities of railways bring about. One day I met a gentleman who had come to Moffat with his family for a month and ... had actually brought the family cow along with them, as he heard the milk from Moffat generally contained a larger mixture of its water than he approved of. My friend seemed quite proud of his cow, which I hope will, like its owner, derive benefit from the air and water of Moffat.

Moffat should become a rich place soon, for upon a moderate calculation carefully made at least £4,000 per week are spent in Moffat by the visitors for about four months in each year." [248]

MOFFAT.—BEATTOCK HOTEL, within a Few Minutes' Walk of Beattock Railway Station.—This Large and First-class Hotel, situated amidst the Romantic and Picturesque Scenery of Upper Annandale, in close proximity to the Celebrated Watering Place, Moffat Spa, and within easy drive of the Grey Mare's Tail and St Mary's Loch, is much frequented by Tourists, Families, and others, for its Moderate Charges, Comfort, and Cleanliness. Close and Open Carriages.
JOHN SINCLAIR *Proprietor.*

Announcement in *The Scotsman* 1869 [249]

1869 There was now a groundswell of dissatisfaction with the state of some things in Moffat and a correspondent called "A Second Year's Visitor"

Eminent Engineers

Joseph Locke (1805-1860), the youngest son of a colliery manager, was born near Sheffield. He was apprenticed to the railway engineer George Stephenson and formed a lifelong friendship with Stephenson's son Robert. Locke, Brunel and Robert Stephenson were to dominate the engineering world.

In 1836 Locke was asked to make preliminary surveys to find the best route for reaching Glasgow and Edinburgh from Carlisle. The obvious solution was to follow Thomas Telford's coach road through Annandale and Clydesdale but Locke did not believe a locomotive could climb the hills to Beattock Summit and his preferred line was a longer one through Nithsdale. However he was persuaded to resurvey the Annandale option and he concluded that it was a practical route after all. When the Caledonian main line opened in 1849 it was possible to travel from London to Glasgow, by express, without needing to change trains.

Joseph was a frequent visitor to Moffat during the 1850s, from where he went shooting on the hills above Beattock. On 12th August 1860 he went to Moffat, where he was joined as usual by a group of friends. He was in good health until, on 17th September, he complained of feeling ill. He died of a ruptured appendix the following day at Mr. And Mrs. Cranstoun's hotel (the Annandale Arms).

According to Locke's biographer "The kind people of Moffat, told that they would see no more the pleasant form they knew so well, testified their grief in simple fashion, closed their shops, congregated in knots, and looked very grave".

Thomas Bouch (1822-1880) was born at Thursby in Cumberland. At the age of seventeen he worked with Joseph Locke on the construction of the Lancaster and Carlisle Railway. By 1873 Thomas was in charge of the construction of a bridge over the River Tay. At the time this was Britain's largest single engineering project and in 1878 the bridge was opened following a painstaking inspection by the Board of Trade. Thomas was knighted by Queen Victoria.

On 28th December 1879 a violent storm caused the collapse of the bridge while a train was crossing and 75 lives were lost. An inquiry did not apportion blame for the disaster, but one of the panel members, in a separate report, placed the blame on Thomas.

These events affected his health and in July 1880 he retired prematurely to Moffat, where he lived in total seclusion with Lady Bouch. After appearing to make a recovery he died of a chest infection at Ellerbank, Moffat on 30th October 1880.

wrote in the following terms to the *Moffat Times*. The youth of Moffat received the brunt of the blame (plus ça change):

"I would wish, as a visitor, to draw attention to one or two matters in connection with a place I have liked so much. The state of the footpaths is disgusting in the extreme and most offensive to the senses, and rarely can one take a walk without becoming polluted; for it would seem as if the dirty perpetrators had a direct purpose in this worst of practical jokes .... surely Moffat, Queen of the Scottish Spas, will not suffer herself to lie under such a reproach. It is presumed that when the sanitary arrangements are otherwise so good, the cottages are provided with necessary accommodation. I suspect the boys are the great offenders, and surely they can be prevented.

Again, why is rubbish of all kinds permitted to be thrown into the Annan and Well Burn, thus destroying the beauty of the streams and rendering them unsightly. Particularly offensive is the habit at the butchers' shambles to throw the intestines into the river.

While the tradespeople and lodging-house keepers are remarkable for their obliging civility, I must find great fault with the boys, who are a rude, unmannerly set. Several cases I have witnessed in which boys up the Annan have teased young gentlemen for hooks, and their refusing (having none) have been assailed with sticks and stones. Only the other day a lad used the most blasphemous swearing because my son could not give him a hook. Parents and schoolmasters should look to this, especially the swearing, which I do not expect to hear in Scotland.

Why have we not a better vegetable and poultry market, and why will the obliging butchers not ... cut up their meat into its proper divisions, shoulders, and legs? Why is there such a scarcity of beef? It would also be a great boon if hotels would keep more saddle-horses during the season. Why are pony excursions not organised, with guides? Moffat requires a regular Band to be supported by the town and by subscriptions from visitors. Many lodging-house keepers

139

know that several visitors left because they found the place
so dull." [250]

1869 Things were clearly hotting up in Moffat, and "Edina" immediately got
out her pen and paper to write the following letter in support of "A
Second Year's Visitor":

"In no part of the three Kingdoms have I ever met with
such an uncivil set of young barbarians as these boys of
Moffat. I have not been able to allow my children to use
ponies during this summer's residence in Moffat owing to
the conduct of these boys last year. Sticks and stones were
thrown at a pony when my little girl was on its back; sly
pinches behind when my children have been resting on a
wall; and swill from a pig tub thrown on them when walking
quietly on the road, are specimens of the treatment they
have received. If this state of things goes on unchequed (*sic*)
parents will be driven to seek safer summer quarters than the
hills and lanes of Moffat." [251]

1870 On 1st October Thomas Woodall, a grocer from Silloth, was found
dead in the Baths Hall. He had gone for a bath after 10.00 p.m. when
he fell ill and drowned in fifteen inches of bath water. [252]

1872 William Black, a novelist from Glasgow, wrote a piece which contains a
description of the town. Although this is fiction, it is clear that William
was familiar with Moffat:

"When we went out for a lounge after luncheon, we
discovered that if Moffat is to be likened to Baden-Baden, it
forms an exceedingly Scotch and respectable Baden-Baden.
The building in which the mineral waters are drunk looks
somewhat like an educational institution, painted white, and
with prim white iron railings. Inside .... we found a long and
sober-looking reading-room. Moffat itself is a white, clean,
wide-streeted place, and the hills around it are smooth and
green, but it is very far removed from Baden-Baden. It is a
good deal more proper, and a great deal more dull. Perhaps
we did not visit it in the height of the season, if it has got a
season; but we were at all events not very sorry to get away
from it again, and out into the hilly country beyond." [253]

1872   In July "A Subscribing Visitor" wrote this rather peevish letter to *The Moffat Times* to complain about the state of the balls of Beechgrove:

> "Sir, - ... I would suggest that the proprietors of the croquet ground should keep the things in order; a more disgraceful set of balls I have never played with. I have searched through all the boxes, and have found, at the outside, three balls that are rendered almost useless from pieces knocked out of them.
>
> The three balls that may be called round have no distinguishing colour to speak of, all having been washed away. Were the bowlers to be presented with balls such as the croquet players have to put up with, how many subscribers would there be to the bowling green? It is but a poor pleasure for a good croquet player to use such tools as are supplied him at the Beechgrove grounds." [254]

1872   Another letter to *The Moffat Times* was signed "Girl of the Period", but one suspects that the writer was in fact a parent of the dusty visitor. The writer comes very close to becoming the first visitor to complain about good weather in Moffat:

> "Oh! Dear Mr. Editor, do they *never* water the streets of this nice little town of Moffat? Mamma sends me out shopping every morning, and when the wind is blowing in the very least I come home covered with nasty dust. It fills my ears and nose, my "Dolly Varden" skirt is full of it, and worst of all, my last new "chignon" (it's a stunner and cost a fortune at Sturrock's just before we left Edinbro') is nearly ruined by it, and mamma is so cross if I ask for a new one. So please do, Mr. Editor, order the streets to be *well watered every morning early*, or I do declare I shall tell mamma she must do her shopping herself, and buy her sugar and strawberries as full of nasty dust as the Moffat people like to sell them. Don't please print this note ...." [255]

1872   Perhaps encouraged by the growing welter of complaints, another visitor, "J.D.", raised his pen to *The Moffat Times*. There is not the space here to quote the entire floweriness of this letter but this gives the general flavour and illustrates the fact that local authorities have never been short of suggestions on how best to spend money:

"Sir .... Nature has done so much to beautify this charming locality, that the authorities and inhabitants generally are apt to think that there is nothing left for them to do. I need scarcely remind you that it is very different with many of the continental watering-places, where considerable sums are spent annually for rendering their natural beauties readily and pleasantly accessible.

Few watering-places possess a tithe of the numerous attractions of Moffat. It is, in truth, a richly-set gem of the first water. Nevertheless, we must bear in mind that a trifling blemish in a fine work pains the eye in proportion to the fineness of the work. It is the pimple in the otherwise perfect face; the stain on that satin dress; the little bit of bad drawing in that fine picture that is certain to arrest the eye, and sadly interfere with the enjoyment of what is truly beautiful. Keeping this truth in mind ... permit me, as a delighted sojourner here for a short time .... to point out several matters which might be rectified at small expense:

Charles Lapworth and the Moffat Series

Charles Lapworth (1842 – 1920) was born on 20th September 1842 at Faringdon in Berkshire. He trained as a school teacher and in 1864 he took up a teaching post at Galashiels. His holidays and spare time were spent wandering over the Border region, and in about 1866 or 1867 he became interested in geology.

At that time the Southern Uplands were known to be made of greywacke rocks, similar to those of the Lake District and Wales. These rocks were thought to be a single series five miles (26,000 feet) thick. At intervals there were bands of black shale, never more than five or six hundred feet thick, which yielded almost the only fossils, chiefly graptolites. The same graptolites were found at every level through the whole five-mile thickness of rock. If this interpretation was correct then the graptolites had stood still, in evolutionary terms, for a long period of time. This was in contradiction of the theory of evolution which was gaining support in geological circles.

Lapworth began detailed fieldwork in the Moffat area in 1869 and he prepared a series of detailed maps covering an area of 30 square miles. He found that the bands of black shale did in fact contain different fossils. At Dobb's Linn, where he stayed at Birkhill, Lapworth divided the Moffat shale into three main groups – Glenkiln, Hartfell, and Birkhill shales - each of which yielded different types of fossils. He then tested his ideas by describing the shales in Upper Annandale, Hartfell, and the Frenchland Burn. The great thickness of the rocks of the area was in fact due to a complex history whereby similar rocks were folded over one another.

Lapworth published his findings in 1878 in a paper entitled *The Moffat Series*. His paper had a mixed reception and met with the incredulity, and even hostility, of the older members of the geological community. Very soon, however, his work was recognised as the basis of future work. Lapworth described his detailed approach to geology as "an advance as rapid as those brought about by the use of the microscope in the history of biology".

In 1881 Lapworth was appointed Professor of Geology at the University of Birmingham and he received every honour that was available from the wider geological community.

In 1984 Dobb's Linn was designated by the International Union of Geological Sciences as the Global Stratotype Section and Point (GSSP) for the boundary between the Ordovician and Silurian.

i] There is a great need for finger-posts to indicate the various routes and the direction and distance of the numerous objects of interest in the vicinity.

ii] The Bridge in front of the Beld Craig, and the seats in the glen are in a very forlorn condition, and should be repaired at once.

iii] The building at the Well, called the "Ball-room" is somewhat of an eyesore. Could it not be put to some useful purpose?

iv] The iron fence should be continued, or a hand rail of some kind put along the footpath overhanging the Well-burn at the Well.

v] A very fine view is obtained from the Lady's Knowe, reminding one, it is said, of Nice. There used to be a seat at the old thorn tree close by, which might with advantage be restored.

vi] That part of the favourite Old Well Road above Havelock Terrace is not in good order and the wall or dyke on the east side is tumbling, to the danger of passers-by.

vii] The road leading through the "Whins", behind the Grammar School, is in a disgraceful state. There is a dung heap on the verge of it, which should be looked after by the police or sanitary commissioners." [256]

1873 Joseph Lister, the pioneer of sterile surgery, and his brother Arthur had visited Moffat with their father when they were young. When Joseph and his wife Agnes were in Moffat in September 1873 they stayed at Mrs. Hamilton's in Old Well Road (this house may have been Elmhill, of which Agnes Hamilton was the proprietor). On 10th September he wrote from Mrs. Hamilton's to his brother:

"My Dear Arthur,
Thee will be surprised to see the above address. We came here yesterday, that I may write a paper which I have promised to the Editor of the *Microscopical Journal*. And most charming this place now is, so different from its appearance as *we* knew it. Now the little gardens are full of bright flowers, the trees in full unimpaired summer foliage, the corn fields golden with the late harvest, the lower hills

emerald green, and the higher ones purple with heather-blossom. I have today been (with Aggie) meditating on the Gallow's Hill, where *fungi* are evidently in profusion. It seems but yesterday that thee and I were there together: and Agnes pointed out to me the scattered scales of a fir cone, no doubt the work of one of thy beloved crossbills.

Now having had lunch and a little quietness after it, we propose to stroll out again and (I daresay by the banks of the Moffat) combine work at my paper with the enjoyment of this charming scenery. Our cottage is very near Hartfell House which is full." [257]

MOFFAT.—Furnished House for One Month or longer. Ten Apartments; pleasant situation. Apply to Wm. Muir & Son.

MOFFAT.—Wm. Muir & Co., House Agents, supply all information regarding Furnished Houses and Lodgings. Pianos on Hire.

MOFFAT.—To Let, Furnished, Country House, Parlour and 3 Bed-Rooms, with Kitchen, &c. Apply to Wm. Muir & Co., Moffat.

MOFFAT.—Craigieburn Farm House to Let, Furnished, Two Sitting, Seven Beds, Stable and Coach-House, Knight, House-Agent.

MOFFAT:—Robert Knight, Bookseller and House Agent, supplies all information regarding Houses and Lodgings. Pianos on Hire.

MOFFAT.—Self-contained Cottage (Elmhill)—2 Parlours, 1 Double and 4 Single Bed Rooms, with Servants' accommodation, Bath, Gas, and Water. Also, FARM-HOUSE (Woodhead), a mile and half from Moffat—2 Parlours, 3 Bed-Rooms, with use of Kitchen and Pony's Grass. Apply James Edgar, Flesher, Moffat.

MOFFAT.—Amos House to Let, Furnished, for July and August, and September if desired, containing Dining, Breakfast, and Drawing-Rooms, Library, Day Nursery, 9 Bed-Rooms (12 beds), Dressing Room with Bath, Bath-Room, Butler's Pantry, Hot and Cold Water and Gas, 3-Stalled Stable, Coachhouse, and Coachman's Room, Large Flower Garden and Croquet Lawn, &c., &c. Apply R. Knight, House Agent.

Announcement in *The Scotsman* 1875 [258]

1874 Stephen Mitchell, a retired tobacco magnate, died on 21st April 1874 following a fall. At the time of his death he was lodging at Floral Cottage. He was seen walking near Archbank and when he did not return a search was carried out by the police and others. His body was found at the bottom of a precipice about 150 yards beyond the well. There was a seat at the top of the precipice and it is probable that he fell about fifty feet from there to the rocks below.

"Stephen Mitchell retired from business in 1869 and he chose to spend his later days in Moffat. Here some of his happiest hours were spent in the back-room of a bookseller's shop (probably Thomas Fairfoul's shop in the High Street), where a subscription library was housed. Mr. Mitchell died while taking a walk to the Wells. His will contained a bequest of a sum amounting to £66,998 10s. 6d. which was to be put out to interest to £70,000 and used for the establishment of a free library for the City of Glasgow, managed by a committee of the town council." [259]

The library was to be known as the Mitchell Library, and no books were to be excluded on the grounds of contravening "present opinions on politics or religion". The Mitchell Library was opened to the public in November 1877, initially with 14,432 volumes. Since its opening in 1877, the Mitchell has grown into one of Europe's largest public reference libraries with a book stock of 1.3 million books, 35,000 maps and thousands of photographs, newspapers and microfilms.

1874   "J.D." wrote yet again to the *Moffat Times* with an alarming view of the greed, avarice, and short-sightedness of the people of Moffat. He also had lots of suggestions on how to improve the town. His concluding idea was to be implemented in the near future:

"It is true that the crowds come – and will come – in spite of many little annoyances and discomforts; but I blush to think of the oft-invoked dissatisfaction at our Scotch niggardliness and short-sighted economy, in which the natives here, from the meanest lodging-house keeper up to the lord of the manor, seem to be steeped to their eyes. The knowledge will come some day but meantime lodging-house economy, meanness and greed rule and guide the destiny of our chief watering-place.

The only additional suggestion I have to offer ... is that we might very effectively relieve the nakedness of the High Street by taking a leaf out of the book of our continental friends, and planting a little in the Boulevard style. Suppose we plant a single or a double line of trees along the east side, and a single line to correspond with the trees already lining the west side from the Annandale Arms inn north." [260]

DUMFRIESSHIRE.

MOFFAT, DUMFRIESSHIRE, N. B.
HOTEL FOR SALE.
There will be Exposed to Sale by Public Roup, at the Upset Price
of £4000, within the Premises, on Friday, 19th November next,
at Two o'clock Afternoon,
The ANNANDALE ARMS HOTEL, situated in the rising and
fashionable Watering-Place of MOFFAT.
The Hotel has good House accommodation, extensive Stabling,
with Coach-Houses, Yard, &c., also a Large Garden, and every
convenience for carrying on a First-class Business, offering a good
Investment for Hotel Keepers and others.
For further particulars apply to the Proprietor, JOHN PROUD-
FOOT, Esq., Ivy House, or to THOMAS TAIT, Solicitor, Moffat, in
whose hands are the Articles of Sale and Titles.
Moffat, 13th October 1875.

Notice in *The Scotsman* 1875 [261]

1874 William Johnstone of Royal Terrace, Edinburgh carried out the latest in a long series of analyses of the waters of the Well. By this time, the techniques which were available for chemical analysis were much improved and the distinctive smell of the water was quantified as being due to the presence of 5.325 cubic centimetres of hydrogen sulphide per litre of water. [262]

1876 An unnamed correspondent wrote a letter, couched in most indignant terms, to express his disgust at what he saw for sale in one of Moffat's shops:

"I am a fisherman of more experience than I care to mention ... The real enemies of sport are not the worthy brethren of the craft, but the greedy pirates that infest some of the best angling localities, such as Moffat, and who clear the rivers of trout for miles round, with nets, during the night and early morning. Having visited the above town *(Moffat)* some time since, I was disgusted at seeing hundreds of trout every morning in a shop window for sale, while no honest angler could by his legitimate art procure one. I need scarcely say that I never went there again to fish." [263]

1878 Moffat Hydro opened and the following account appeared in September of that year:

"The Hydropathic Establishment at Moffat, situated by train an hour from Carlisle, is on a large scale. Besides Billiard and Recreation rooms, it has accommodation for three hundred

Notice in *The Scotsman* 1878 [264]

visitors. The pleasure-grounds extend to twenty-five acres.
The bath arrangements are most complete, comprising
Turkish, swimming, and every other description. Moffat
Well, a popular spa, is in the vicinity.

In this gigantic concern, the charge for board, lodgings,
baths etc. is from £2 12s. 6d. to three guineas each person
per week. The Establishment was opened only a few months
ago; and the average attendance of visitors, as we
understand, has been two hundred persons daily. The outlay
on the undertaking has been so far on a magnificent scale,
amounting to fifty-five thousand pounds. The entire cost
will probably be seventy thousand pounds." [265]

1881 The following letter appeared in *The Scotsman*, dated 16th May and
signed by "W.S.":

Sir, - Last week when on a fishing trip to St. Mary's Loch, I
was surprised as well as delighted when told on arriving that
an osprey had been about the loch for some days. In the
evening, when taking a turn by the Loch o' the Lowes, it
rose from an old tree on the hill-side, and after hovering
about for some time, disappeared behind the Ettrick hills.

Next morning, about half-past eight, when driving by the
side of Loch o' the Lowes, *en route* to Loch Skene, it rose
from the same place, and again was lost to view behind the
hills opposite Meggat Waterfoot. On arriving at Loch Skene
at ten, an osprey rose and soared about the loch the most of

the day. When we returned to Tibbie's at four o'clock, we were told that the osprey had been there also; and two Englishmen, resplendent in knickerbockers and shooting caps, donned, no doubt, for the occasion, proudly informed us that they had succeeded in getting a couple of shots at it (happily without doing any harm).

When we left that night, the knickerbockered strangers were stalking about, gun in hand, in the morbid hope of again having a shot at it. Whether the one at St. Mary's and the one at Loch Skene were the same or not I could not be sure, although I am inclined to think they were different. Where they came from I know not, but up till within twenty years or so, a pair built their nests on the rocky islet at the south end of Lock Skene. – I am, Etc." [266]

1882   Abel Heywood Junior published what is perhaps one of the most evocative pieces of travel writing about Moffat. Anyone who has returned to Moffat after a long stay in other parts will recognise the sights and feelings described by Abel:

"If one could only get into the North train at Victoria Station at 1.15 a.m., to be a little after midnight in endless, monotonous, wearisome streets, and at breakfast time to find oneself, after an unconscious journey, at Moffat, one of the sweetest little towns in Her Majesty's dominions. Moffat air will make you forget your fretful and restless night, and drooping eyes will never remind you, even as night comes on again, that you have been forty hours without rest.

To attempt to describe your sensations as you emerge from the station *(Beattock)* and climb on to the 'bus, must result in miserable failure. As the bus rolls on its way, how delightful is every remembered object that comes in view – the square black inn with its pillared porch – the old square Scottish tower, and the Roman way that runs by it but no trace of which you have been able to find – every rise and fall of the road – every tree – every changeful outline of the hills – all there as they were, just as if *you* had not been away for ever so many years. Now you cross the straight little river, and see the blue smoke of your own town wreathing at the foot of the dark wooded hill beyond, now you enter the street, pass the Black Bull, you are under the shade of the giant elm trees that front the old church, then you turn sharp round unto the market place, around which the town is gathered; the 'bus stops, you are immediately in the hospitable entrance of the Buccleuch Arms, and after a souse in the bedroom, come down to breakfast "as fresh as paint", and your holiday has begun.

What a charm there is in re-visiting a spot you have come to know and love. How intimate do you find your memory to be, as you gaze out of the window and recognise, almost with a smile and a nod as though they were old acquaintances, the bricks and mortar which in the main seem to be exactly as you left them. How ready is your eye to note the town "improvements" – disfigurements as they seem to you – for how could the old place be better than as you first knew it, when it consisted of little more than the one great street or square of whitewashed houses, and one or two off-streets, where the few detached lodging houses were located? A clean simple, delightful little town was Moffat twenty years ago. The extensions and improvements have no charm for you. But it cannot be helped; the march of events will not spare even Moffat; and with this trace of sadness in your joy, you sit down to breakfast." [267]

In June, "Nautilus" set off on a 69-day, 2,462 mile, journey across the length and breadth of Scotland. He began his travels with a friend who dropped out somewhere in the Highlands. Perhaps this was not altogether unexpected because they had chosen to travel by pedal tricycle. Nautilus deserves his place in this volume if only because he was one of the very few to complain about good weather in the Moffat area. The 15th of June, the fourth day of his journey, found him in Moffat after he and his colleague, in the footsteps of Sir Walter Scott, had climbed up to Loch Skene:

> "And, gentle reader, I tell you in the strictest confidence that we felt rather angry with poor Sir Walter for having caused us this fatigue and delay by his description of grandeur which we failed to discover. The fact is that the peculiarities of the lake are only to be seen when the sky is dark and obscured, whereas on the present occasion the evening was bright and clear .... the town *(Moffat)*, embosomed in hills, looked very pretty as we approached. Right glad we were to find comfortable quarters at the "Star" at 9 p.m."

On the 68th day of his journey, Nautilus was again in Moffat:

> "I now came to the Devil's Beeftub, a deep precipitous dell, the source of the River Annan. Here I had a vista of the green vale to Moffat, resting prettily among the trees. On approaching the town, a change came o'er the spirit of the place. My path no longer led me over the bleak and lonely mountain, but ran by shady trees, where ladies were seated here and there with novels in their hands. By-and-by I passed gay groups of tennis players, actively endeavouring to keep the ball going over the net, while scattered couples were apparently very pleasantly engaged in the more secluded corners of the ground. At 3.15 p.m. I was cordially greeted by my hostess of the "Star" who was much interested in hearing of my adventures since last we met." [268]

1884 James John Hissey undertook a thousand-mile trip through England and Scotland. A horse and trap was his chosen conveyance and he must therefore have had a much more comfortable journey than "Nautilus". However, one senses some boredom with his stay at the

Hydro and this may explain his rather crotchety assessment of the rest of Moffat as he was leaving town:

"At Moffat we took up our quarters at the Hydropathic Establishment, a fine building well situated on a height close to the town. Here we managed to put through a week very well, but a week was enough for us, and we were not sorry to re-commence our journey.

The people who patronised the Establishment all appeared to enjoy most excellent health: certainly they did not seem in any way to belong to the invalid or delicate class. We had fairly-acted charades and somewhat tame dances in the evening, everyone appearing to dance to a step of his own particular choosing. What with lawn-tennis, bowls, mountain rambles, excursions and baths all day long, everybody's time was well occupied; on wet days the baths appeared to be a great resource.

We drove along through the village of Moffat, past the pretty lawn-tennis and croquet grounds, past the market-place, with its curious drinking-fountain in the centre, on past its ugly churches, and - no offence to any gallant Scotchman - they do know how to build ugly churches in the "North Countrie", and so on to the fair county roads." [269]

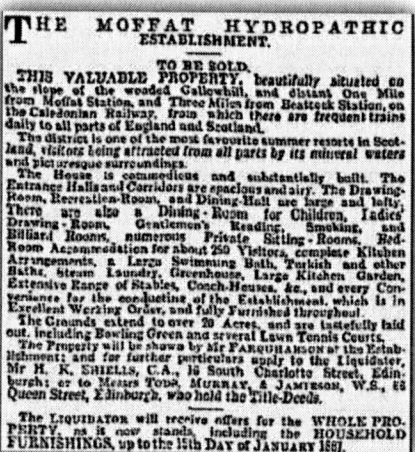

Announcement in *The Scotsman* 1886 [270]

152

1896 William Allan, Member of Parliament for Gateshead-on-Tyne, was a great admirer of Moffat and he and his family were regular holiday visitors. Mr. Knight, the bookseller in Moffat, had recently published an album of photographic views of Moffat and he sent a copy to William, who was moved to take up his pen and write the following lines:

> "The souvenir you kindly sent,
> O' Moffat's bonny views,
> Will aye a charm to me present
> An' kittle up my muse;
> The hills, the dales, the waterfa's,
> The streams to me so dear,
> O' a' my longin' aye the cause,
> When far from them I steer.
>
> The quiet hush, the cosy cots,
> The solemn wuds' aroon',
> The purlin' brooks, the flowery spots,
> The birds wi' hearts in tune,
> A' show 'twas part o' nature's plan
> That here the heart and eyes
> O' weary waefu', toil-worn man
> Mind find a Paradise." [271]

Announcement in *The Scotsman* 1896 [272]

1897 On Saturday 18th September, a motor car passed through Moffat and "created quite a sensation". [273] The first motor car to run on a British road had been a 2 h.p. Benz Velo in November 1894. The great days of the horse drawn coach had gone and those of the local railway were now numbered. Things were about to change again, not necessarily for the worse and not necessarily for the better.

1897 An unnamed writer to the Glasgow *Evening News* was another enthusiastic supporter of Moffat and he recommended it to an earlier correspondent to the newspaper who had signed himself "Rheumatic":

"Why this (Moffat), the sweetest and cleanest of Scottish towns has been hitherto so much neglected passes my comprehension. The scenery is lovely, there are numberless short walks of great beauty close to the town, in strong contrast to most country places where walks are restricted to half-a-dozen perhaps. Visitors are free to roam over the heather-clad hills and moors; there are five or six excellent trout streams where the fishing is quite free. The finest roads in the kingdom for bicycling are found near Moffat.

The water supply and sanitary arrangements are the best, and the railway fares are very moderate. From my own experience I can heartily recommend Moffat and its sulphur springs to "Rheumatic", having derived very great benefit from them for nearly seventeen years, surely a strong recommendation, as there are but few places on which one would care to spend summer holidays for seventeen years as I have done." [274]

RESIDENCE AT MOFFAT.

For SALE by Public Roup, within the Faculty Hall, Glasgow, on Wednesday, 24th January 1900, at Two o'clock Afternoon, unless previously Sold privately,

HOPE LODGE, MOFFAT, a Beautiful and Substantial Residence, containing 4 Public Rooms, 10 Bed-Rooms, 2 Dressing-Rooms, Ample Servants' Accommodation, and all Modern Conveniences. The Grounds, extending to about an Acre and a quarter, are tastefully laid out and furnished with well-grown Shrubs and Trees; Garden, Greenhouse, &c. The Office -Houses comprise a Three-Stalled Stable, Coach-House, Kennel, &c. The situation is near Railway Station, is well sheltered, and commands an excellent view.

For further particulars apply to A. & J. C. ALLAN & Co., Solicitors, Falkirk, who will exhibit the Titles and Articles of Roup.

Notice in *The Scotsman* 1899 [275]

1899 The following account of Moffat provides a fitting and thoughtful conclusion to the 19th Century. This visitor certainly did not believe that things had changed for the better:

"The passing of one generation has transformed Moffat from the quiet little pastoral town, with its white-washed, often thatched, cottages, into the modern gay summer resort. With its fashionable costumes, lawn tennis ground, pretentious villas straggling far up its glens, and the inevitable Hydropathic stranded like Noah's Ark betwixt the peaks of Ararat. In the old time you reached it by coach; now the railway is in the heart of it. Then the villagers had their common grazing for the cows which came solemnly home in a troop at nightfall, one by one turning into her own pend until the old herd saw the last safely housed; now the bustle and chatter of the tourists are everywhere.

The kirks have felt the change in the times, and have forsaken the primitive seclusion of back wynds, and vie with one another in the magnificence of their Gothic and the heights of their spires. And the manses, with the old-fashioned gardens that told more of the kail-pot than of floral decorations, have given place to mansions that would have been royal palaces to the Johnstones in the reiver days. Edinburgh lawyers and Glasgow magnates call for their city comforts among the hills nowadays, and Moffat has to live by suiting the tastes of its patrons. Ah! well; some of us think the air was more caller and the simple fare sweeter in the old days." [276]

New Year's Eve and New Year's Day 1899-1900

After much national debate it was finally settled that the 20th Century would begin with the year 1900 and not with 1901. New Year's day fell on a Monday.

The occasion was recorded by the *Moffat News*:

"As on previous occasions, a small knot of young people awaited the arrival of New Year on the High Street, and gave hearty cheers as the clock pealed the hour. The old custom of "first-footing" was kept up, and in the early morning quite a number of calls were made, and the usual greetings exchanged.

A service was held in the hall of the Free Church, when the Rev. K. Moody Stuart and the Rev. Somerville Reid

155

officiated. In the Established Church the Sabbath School children, numbering two hundred, gathered together, along with their teachers and a few friends. The Rev. R. Somers B.D., conducted the service, at the conclusion of which the children were each made the recipient of a bun and an orange. The United Presbyterian Church Sabbath School children also had their annual treat, when the Rev. J. Todd, pastor of the congregation, conducted a children's service. There was a good attendance. In the Episcopal Church services were held, and the Rev. John Molony officiated with much acceptance.

The day was observed as a general holiday, and all the shops and offices were closed. The drapers also shut their shops on the Tuesday. There was a very large number of visitors in the town, and the Hydro was unusually well patronised. While there was a large influx of visitors, there was a good number of natives who left by the morning trains for Glasgow and Edinburgh. The town presented a lively appearance, the weather being of a fine bracing nature, and thus affording an opportunity to most people of being out of doors. The posting establishments were exceptionally busy, a large proportion of the visitors going for drives in the district.

Notwithstanding the heavy rainfall on Saturday, the ice on Dumcrieff Pond was pretty firm after the hard frost which prevailed on Sunday night, and this pond was the scene of an enthusiastic gathering of curlers and skaters. A counter attraction to the ice was a football match on the Cricket Field between the Dalziel Rovers and Moffat Harriers, which resulted in the victory of the former by 7–1. In the evening a fancy dress ball was held, and was attended with success.

Taken as a whole New Year's Day here was quite up to former years, and we have no doubt that the visitors would go away invigorated with their visit to Moffat." [277]

Posts, Telegraphs and Telephones

The ability to transmit messages quickly and reliably has been important throughout history. As trade in Moffat increased and visitors arrived from the business and professional classes, access to effective methods of communication became an essential part of the local infrastructure.

Telegraphy is the long-distance transmission of messages without the physical transport of letters. On the basis of this definition the first recorded use of telegraphy in Moffat was the use of bale fires. A Scottish Act of Parliament in 1455 directed that one bale of fire should be lit to warn of the approach of the English in any manner; two bales blazing, that they are coming indeed; and four bales, that they are coming in great force. A chain of beacons was established from the Border in the south to Annandale. The sites included "Bleis" Hill in Wamphray, "Kindol-knok" in Johnstone and the Gallow Hill by Moffat.

Moffat's early postal service consisted of carriers who rode between "posts" where the postmaster would remove the letters for the local area before handing back the remaining letters and any additions. However, the letters were often carried by irresponsible lads on old worn out horses and the service was irregular and unreliable. The introduction of the new mail coach service to Moffat in 1788 was a revolution and it continued until 1848 when it was superseded by the railway. Hotel proprietors at that time acted as postmasters.

Moffat's first official post office was in Well Street in the building later occupied by Hepburn's bakers shop. Thomas Grieve was the postmaster in 1841 and 1851 and he was succeeded by his daughter, Marion Grieve. By the late 1860s the post office had moved to the High Street, two doors north of the British Linen Bank (Arden House). Ann Black was the postmistress for many years until the 1890s when Margaret Grieve took over. The new post office opened at its current site on 8th June 1900.

Moffat's first electrical Telegraph Office was opened on 5th February 1870. The telegraph posts and wires ran by the side of the Beattock Road then along the bank of the Annan to Crooks before entering the town along Reid's Entry. The telegraph office was part of the Post Office. The first telephone exchange in Moffat opened on 28th August 1901 as part of the new Post Office.

Moffat Hydropathic and Pension [278]

TERMS, &c.

| | 7/6 | 8/6 |
Board, Baths, &c., according to Bedroom, per day, { 9/6 10/6

Two occupying one Bed, according to Bedroom, each,
per day, ... 9/- 10-
Children under Ten years of age by arrangement.
Over ten, 5/- per day in Nursery; 6/- in Dining
Room.

Visitors' Servants, ... per day, 0 5 0
During August 1/- per day additional to above rates.
Visitors for less than a week, 1/- a day extra.

BREAKFAST at 8.30 A.M.; LUNCHEON at 1.30 P.M.; AFTERNOON
TEA between 4 and 5 P.M.; DINNER at 7 P.M.; TEA AND COFFEE
immediately after.

Breakfast served out of the Public Room, extra for
each person, ... 0 0 6
Dinner served out of the Public Room, extra for
each person, ... 0 1 0
Charges for Visitors' friends. Breakfast, 2/-; Lunch, 2/-;
Dinner, 3/6.
Attendance is included in the above charges.
Wine may be used at table, at visitors' discretion.

Private Parlours, ... per day, 0 9 0
Fire in Private Room, ... per day, 0 1 6
Fire in Bedroom, ... per day, 0 1 3
Fire in ,, ... per evening, 0 0 9
Day of arrival charged. Day of departure free.
Accounts to be settled weekly.
An excellent Laundry attached to the Establishment.
Good Accommodation for Bicycles.
No dogs allowed in the House.

VISITING PHYSICIAN.

T. B. WHITE, M.B., C.M., Dickson House, High Street.

DAVID HUSKIE, M.B., C.M., Hamilton House, Well Road, may
also attend Visitors to the Establishment at their request.

JOHN FARQUHARSON,
Secretary.

Moffat's entry in the National Telephone Directory of 1904 - 1905

MOFFAT AREA.
MOFFAT EXCHANGE.

0713 CALEDONIAN Railway Co.	.. ..	Moffat station
0716 DEANE F. D. W...	.. ..	Dundanion Moffat
0714 FINGLAND A. ..	.. ..	Buccleuch hotel
0720 HETHERINGTON J., Chemist	.. ..	High st
706 HUSKIE Dr. D., Medical Practitioner		Hamilton ho
0719 LAIDLAW A., Butcher	.. ..	Well rd
708 McDONALD D. & J., Hotelkeepers		Annandale Arms htl
0715 MILLAR J., Draper ..	.. ..	High st
707 MOFFAT Hydropathic	.. (Office)	Beechgrove Moffat
707a do. Hydropathic ..	(Call Box)	Beechgrove Moffat
709 POST Office (for Postal facilities only)		High st
0717 WEATHERHEAD J., Baker	.. ..	High st
0718 YOUNG J., Grocer, Spirit Merchant	..	High st

158

Sources and Biographical Notes

1   *Eastern Dumfriesshire: an archaeological landscape.* Royal Commission on the Ancient and Historical Monuments of Scotland (HMSO, 1997)

2   *The Life of Gnaeus Julius Agricola.* Cornelius Tacitus.

3   *The Last Frontier: the Roman Invasions of Scotland.* Antony Kamm. (Tempus Publishing, Stroud, 2004)

4   *The Quest for Merlin.* Nicolai Tolstoy (Sceptre, London, 1988)

5   *Moffat ..... A Backward Glance.* Sheila Forman (Lochar Publishing, Moffat, 1949)

6   *Arthur and the Lost Kingdoms.* Alistair Moffat (Weidenfeld & Nicolson, London, 1999)

7   *The Actes and Deidis of the Illustre and Vallyeant Campioun Schir William Wallace.* Blind Harry or Henry the Minstrel (about 1477)

8   *Fons Moffatensis; seu Descriptio, Topigraphico-Spagyrica, Fontium Mineralium Moffetensium in Annandia Scotiae.* Matthew Mackaile. (Edinburgh, 1659)

    Moffet Well or A topigraphico spagyricall description of the Mineral Wells at Moffet in Annandale of Scotland. Matthew Mackaile. (Robert Brown, Edinburgh, 1664)

    Matthew Mackaile (? - ?) was a surgeon and apothecary from Aberdeen. He had an interest in alchemy.

9   *Medicine, Health and Economic Development: Promoting Spa and Seaside Resorts in Scotland c. 1750-1830 (in Medical History Volume. 47).* Gordon Durie. (Wellcome Trust, London, 2003)

10   *The Social Life of Scotland in the Eighteenth Century.* Henry Grey Graham (A.& C. Black, London, 1899)

11   *The Public Roads and Bridges in Dumfriesshire 1650-1820.* James Robertson. (GC Book Publishers, Wigtown, 1993)

12   *Domestic medicine, or, the family physician: being an attempt to render the medical art more generally useful by shewing people what is in their own power both with respect to the prevention and cure of diseases. Chiefly calculated to recommend a proper attention to regimen and simple medicines.* William Buchan. (Balfour, Auld and Smellie, Edinburgh, 1769)

    William Buchan (1729-1805) was the author of the internationally famous manual *Domestic Medicine*. As a schoolboy he had practised as an amateur doctor among the poor in his native village of Ancrum in Scotland. He graduated MD at Edinburgh in 1761. From 1766, in addition to his medical practice, he lectured on natural philosophy at Edinburgh University. He moved to London in 1788 where he established a large and prosperous practice. Catherine the Great of Russia sent Buchan a gold medal in honour of his work. In 1927 *Domestic Medicine* was still reported to be in frequent use in Scotland.

[13] *Moffat Past and Present.* John Brown (editor of the Moffat Times). (J. Menzies, Edinburgh 1873)

[14] *Medical Reports on the Effects of Water, Cold and Warm, as a remedy in Fevers and other Diseases.* Dr. James Currie (Cadell and Davies, London, 1797)

[15] *The Cold Water Cure, its Principles, Theory, and Practice.* Vincent Priessnitz. (William Strange, London, 1842)

[16] *The Moffat Times, Register and Annandale Observer* 10th April 1858

Samuel Neil (1825–1901), schoolmaster and writer, was born in Edinburgh. He was rector of Moffat Academy from 1855 to 1873 and he was an enormous influence over the development of Moffat as a resort.. Neil combined much literary activity with his work in education. He promoted in 1857, and edited during its existence, the *Moffat Register and Annandale Observer*, the first newspaper published in Moffat, and he wrote regularly for other Scottish periodicals and educational journals. On resigning his rectorship of Moffat Academy in 1873 Neil settled in Edinburgh, devoting himself to English literature, and especially to Shakespeare. He founded and was president of the Edinburgh Shakespeare Society, and gave the annual lecture from 1874 until his death.

[17] *Taking the Water-Cure: The Hydropathic Movement in Scotland, 1840-1940.* James Bradley, Marguerite Dupree, Alastair Durie. Published in *Business and Economic History*, Volume 26, No.2, Winter 1997.

[18] *Dumfries and Galloway Standard* 9th February 1887.

[19] *Delineations, historical, topographical, and descriptive of the watering and sea-bathing places of Scotland.* W. M. Wade (John Lawrence, Paisley,1822)

[20] *The Pennylesse Pilgrimage; or, the Moneylesse Perambulation of John Taylor, alias the Kings Magesties Water-Poet; How He TRAVAILED on Foot from London to Edenborough in Scotland, Not Carrying any Money To or Fro, Neither Begging, Borrowing, or Asking Meate, Drinke, or Lodging.* John Taylor. (E. Allde, London, 1618).

John Taylor (1580-1653), was an English pamphleteer, commonly called the " Water-Poet," because he was employed as a Thames waterman. In 1614 he published the palindrome: "Lewd did I live, & evil I did dwel." An account of his journey, in 1618, from London to Edinburgh appeared in a pamphlet.

[21] *The History of Glasgow.* John McUre (Glasgow, 1830)

Walter Whiteford (? – 1647) was appointed to the ministry at Moffat in 1610 and in 1613 he was nominated to the commission of the peace for Annandale, and was involved in several of the local family feuds. In 1635 Whiteford was consecrated as Bishop of Brechin. The new service book was very unpopular, and in 1637, when Whiteford announced his intention of reading it, he was threatened with violence. Undeterred he ascended the pulpit, holding a brace of pistols, his family and servants attending him in arms, and read the service behind closed doors. On his return he was attacked by an enraged mob, and escaped with difficulty. In 1638 he was deposed and excommunicated by the

Glasgow assembly, whose authority, in common with the other Scottish bishops, he had refused to recognise. He was accused before the assembly of moral turpitude and closet papistry and he fled to England. His daughter Rachel had earlier married James Johnstone, Earl of Corehead.

[22] *The Life of John Buncle, Esq.: Containing Various Observations ... Volume III.* Thomas Amory (London,1770)

[23] *Echoes of the Past.* Rev. William Bennet (MacNiven and Wallace, Edinburgh, 1899)

> **Rev. William Bennet** (1822-1899) was born at Ettrick, the son of John Bennet and Elizabeth Singer. He spent much of his childhood with his mother at Kirkpatrick-Juxta where his grandfather was the minister. Educated at Moffat Academy and Edinburgh he was licensed to preach in 1845 but by 1851 he retired to live with his mother in Moffat where he pursued his literary interests. They lived at Claremont, Old Well Road.

[24] *Annandale Family Book of the Johnstones, Earls and Marquises of Annandale, Volume 1.* Sir William Fraser. (Edinburgh, 1894)

[25] *The Scotts of Buccleuch* Vol.1 page 375: quoted in the *Annandale Family Book of the Johnstones, Earls and Marquises of Annandale, Volume 1.* Sir William Fraser. (Edinburgh, 1894)

[26] *The Letters of Charles Kirkpatrick Sharpe,* as reported in the *Dumfries and Galloway Standard.* 12th December 1889

> **Sir Robert Grierson** (1655 - 1733) inherited the lands of Lag in Dumfriesshire. He married Lady Henrietta Douglas, daughter of James Douglas, 2nd Earl of Queensberry, and sister of William Douglas, later 1st Duke of Queensberry. He was directly responsible for a number of deaths during "The Killing Times".

[27] *Oxford Dictionary of National Biography.*

> **George Sinclair** (? - 1696), natural philosopher and university professor, became professor of philosophy at Glasgow University in 1655 and later professor of mathematics and experimental philosophy. He was associated with the invention of the diving bell.

[28] *The History of the Sufferings of the Church of Scotland, from the Restoration to the Revolution. Volume II.* Rev. Robert Woodrow. (Blackie, Fullarton & Co., Glasgow, 1830)

[29] *Memorials and Letters Illustrative of the Life and Times of John Graham of Claverhouse, Viscount Dundee.* Mark Napier (T.G. Stevenson, Edinburgh, 1862)

[30] *Nuncius Scoto-Britannus, de Descriptione Scotiae Antiquae et Modernae.* Robert Sibbald (Edinburgh, 1683)
Robert Sibbald (?1640 - 1721), was born in Fife. He graduated in medicine at the University of Leyden in 1661 but then gave most of his energy to the study of the natural history, antiquities and topography of Scotland.

[31] *Select Biographies*, edited by William King Tweedie (The Woodrow Society, Edinburgh, 1847)

[32] *The Philosophical Transactions and Collections to the End of the Year MDCC Volume III.* John Lowthorp (Royal Society, London, 1749)

[33] *Wamphray.* John Paterson. (Halliday, 1906)

[34] The 1705 Account was published in *Blackwood's Edinburgh Magazine Volume 2 1817-18.*

[35] *A Journey to Edenborough in Scotland.* Joseph Taylor. Republished by William Cowan (William Brown, Edinburgh, (1903)

[36] *Mr. Simson's Knotty Case: Divinity, Politics, and Due Process in Early 18th Century Scotland.* Anne Skoczylas. (McGill-Queen's Press- MQUP, 2001)

John Simson (1668?-1740) was a Scottish theologian. He was licensed as a minister in 1698 and was called to Troqueer, Kirkcudbrightshire in 1705. In 1708 he was promoted to Professor of Divinity at Glasgow University. From then on his name was a byword as a disseminator of bad doctrine. In 1729 it was deemed that it was "not fit or safe" that he should teach divinity.

[37] *The Journal of Mr. James Hart.* James Hart (Edinburgh, 1832)

James Hart (? - 1720) was a minister of Greyfriars in Edinburgh.

[38] *Moffat: Early Roads and Coaching Days.* Thomas Henderson (Annandale Observer Press, Lockerbie, 1960)

[39] *Remains, Historical and Literary, Connected with the Palatine Counties of Lancaster and Chester.* The Chetham Society (Edinburgh, 1845)

[40] *Annals of Three Dumfriesshire Dales.* W.A.J. Prevost (Herald Press, Lockerbie, 1954)

[41] As related by James Hogg. Printed in The *Moffat Register and Annandale Observer* 6th October 1860.

[42] *A Journey Through Scotland (Volume 3).* John Macky (J. Pemberton, London, 1773)

[43] *A tour thro' the whole island of Great Britain. Divided into circuites or journeys. Giving a particularly entertaining account of Whatever is curious and worth observation. Volume IV.* Daniel Defoe (London, 1762)

Daniel Defoe (1659/1661 – 1731) was a writer, journalist, and spy, who gained enduring fame for his novel *Robinson Crusoe*. Defoe is notable for being one of the earliest practitioners of the novel and helped popularize the genre in Britain. In some texts he is even referred to as one of the founders, if not the founder, of the English novel.

[44] *Memoirs of the Life, Time, and Writings, of the Reverend and Learned Thomas Boston.* Thomas Boston (Murray, Cochrane, & Anderson, Stirling, 1776)

Thomas Boston (1676-1732) was a Scottish church leader who, at the time of his visit to Moffat, was the minister of Ettrick Church. At one time he was famous throughout Scotland for his books and preaching, but his fame never took him to any more important ministry

[45] *The Miscellany of the Third Spalding Club. Volume II.* (Third Spalding Club, Aberdeen, 1940)

George Skene (1695 - 1756) was born into the family which for centuries had owned the lands of Skene, some ten miles inland from Aberdeen. He was annually elected Rector of Marischal College and University, Aberdeen. For each of the years 1737-1745.

[46] *The Monthly Review. Volume 1. New Series.* Charles William Wason (G. Henderson, London, 1837)

[47] *Memoirs of the Life of Sir John Clerk of Penicuik.* John Clerk (T. & A. Constable for the Scottish History Society, 1892)

Sir John Clerk of Penicuik (1676 – 1755) was a Scottish politician, lawyer, judge, composer and architect. He was one of the friends and patrons of the poet Allan Ramsay.

[48] *London Daily Post and General Advertiser* 10th June 1736

[49] *The Journal of William Fordyce.* This extract was published in the *Moffat Times* 24th June 1871

Sir William Fordyce (1724 – 1792) physician, was born at Aberdeen. He became a fellow of the Royal Society in 1787 and was knighted in the same year. William would have been aged only 13 when he made his trip to Moffat. At the time of his death he was Lord Rector of Marischal College, Aberdeen, to which he left his medical library, and where he founded the lectureship on agriculture.

[50] *Memoirs of the Life of Sir John Clerk of Penicuik.* John Clerk (T. & A. Constable for the Scottish History Society, 1892)

[51] This unattributed quotation is provided in *Moffat ..... A Backward Glance.* Sheila Forman (Lochar Publishing, Moffat, 1949)

[52] *Autobiography of the Rev. Dr. Alexander Carlyle, Minister of Inveresk.* Alexander Carlyle (Ticknor & Fields, Cambridge University Press, 1861)

Alexander Carlyle (1722 – 1805) was a Scottish church leader and writer. He witnessed the Battle of Prestonpans in 1745 and in 1770 he became Moderator of the General Assembly. Nicknamed "Jupiter" Carlyle because of his striking physical appearance.

[53] *Oxford Dictionary of National Biography*

[54] *The Scottish Nation: Or, The Surnames, Families, Literature, Honours, and … Volume III.* William Anderson. (Fullarton & Co., Edinburgh, 1863)

Eleanor Dalrymple (ca 1680 - 1759), was the seventh and youngest child of James Campbell, second Earl of Loudoun. Her first husband, Sir James Primrose, subjected Eleanor to marital abuse and their marriage was dissolved following the discovery of his bigamous marriage in Holland. Eleanor later married John Dalrymple, the second Earl of Stair. His heavy drinking was a problem during their early years together; often violent when drunk he hit her in the face one night and woke next day to find her weeping and covered in blood. Overcome with remorse he promised to change his ways and after that she always sat beside him at social events and restricted the amount of wine that he took.

[56] *The Rash Adventurer.* Winifred Duke (Robert Hale, London, 1952)

[57] *Miscellany of the Spalding Club. Volume 1.* (Aberdeen, 1841)

[58] *Annals of Three Dumfriesshire Dales.* W.A.J. Prevost (Herald Press, Lockerbie, 1954)

[59] *Jacobite Memoirs of the Rebellion of 1745.* Robert Forbes. (W.& R. Chambers, Edinburgh, 1834)

[60] *A Journey Through Part of England and Scotland Along with the Army Under the Duke of Cumberland By A Volunteer.* James Ray. (London, 1747)

[61] *An Account of the Virtues and Use of the Mineral Waters near Moffat.* George Milligen. Published in *Medical Essays and Observations….Volume 1* (London, 1746)

[62] *Experiments on the Medicinal Waters of Moffat.* Andrew Plummer. Published in *Medical Essays and Observations Volume 1* (A Society in Edinburgh, Edinburgh, 1752)

Andrew Plummer (1799? - 1756), was educated at Edinburgh and Leyden Universities. In 1722 he set up in practice as a physician in Edinburgh before being appointed Professor of Chemistry and Medicine at Edinburgh University.

[63] Cited in *Moffat 17th to 20th Century.* Jane I. Boyd. (Moffat, 1987)

[64] This diary is quoted, without attribution, in *A Talk on Moffat* (read at the Young Folk Rally of the Well Road U.F. Church, Moffat) by John T. Johnstone, 23rd January 1922.

[65] *Curiosities of a Scots Charta Chest, 1600-1800.* Atholl Forbes, Alexander Dick (W. Brown, Edinburgh, 1897)

[66] *The East Neuk of Fife: its history and antiquities etc.* Walter Wood (Oliver & Boyd, Edinburgh, 1862)

[67] *The Social Life of Scotland in the Eighteenth Century.* Henry Grey Graham (A.& C. Black, London, 1899)

[68] *Experiments and observations upon the Hartfell Spa, made at Moffat 1750; and an account of its medicinal virtues, so far as they have hitherto been discovered from experience.* William Horseborough (Hamilton and Balfour, Edinburgh, 1754)

[69] *Sketch of the Early Life of James Boswell,* written by himself for Jean-Jacques Rousseau. (1765)

James Boswell (1740 - 1795), lawyer, diarist, and author born in Edinburgh. Most famous for his *Life of Samuel Johnson,* published in 1791.

[70] *Boswell's London Journal 1762-1763* (The Reprint Society, London,1952)

[71] *Boswell in Holland 1763-1764 (including his correspondence with Belle de Zuylen).* Edited by Frederick A. Pottle (McGraw-Hill, New York, 2007)

[72] *London Journal.* 9th February 1763, p. 187

[73] *Annals of Three Dumfriesshire Dales.* W.A.J. Prevost (Herald Press, Lockerbie, 1954)

[74] *William Roy Military Survey of Scotland 1747-1755.* National Library of Scotland.

William Roy (1726 - 1790) was born at Miltonhead, near Carluke, He was the son of an estate factor and attended the grammar school at Lanark. He worked for the Post Office in Edinburgh as a surveyor of roads, as well as for the Board of Ordnance as a draughtsman. Roy probably undertook the initial work on the Survey around Fort Augustus and further afield single-handedly. From 1748 he was assisted by six surveying parties, with six men within each survey party; the Highlands were largely complete by 1752, while southern Scotland was completed by 1755.

[75] *Le voyageur François, ou Le connoissance de l'Ancien et du Nouveau monde.* Joseph de Laporte, Louis Domayron, Louis-Abel de Bonafons (L. Cellot, Paris, 1769)

[76] *The Coltness Collections, MDCVIII.-MDCCCXL.* James Dennistoun, Archibald Steuart Denham, Margaret Steuart Calderwood. (Maitland Club,1842)

[77] Ossian is the narrator, and supposed author, of a cycle of poems which the poet James Macpherson claimed to have translated from ancient sources in the Scots Gaelic. In 1760 Macpherson published the English-language text

Fragments of Ancient Poetry collected in the Highlands of Scotland, and later that year obtained further manuscripts. In 1761 he claimed to have found an epic on the subject of the hero Fingal, written by Ossian. The furore over the authenticity of the poems continued into the 20th century.

[78] This verse is attributed to Home, and to Moffat Well, in both History *of Moffat*. W. Robertson Turnbull (W.P. Nimmo, Edinburgh, 1871) and *Moffat ..... A Backward Glance*. Sheila Forman (Lochar Publishing, Moffat, 1949)

   John Home (1722 – 1808), Church of Scotland minister and playwright. The staging of his play *Douglas* sparked a religious controversy. Presbyterian opposition to drama was exacerbated by the circumstances: the dramatist was a clergyman and performances were attended by ministers. Mrs Siddons and David Garrick played parts in his plays.

[79] *Scottish Men of Letters in the Eighteenth Century*. Henry Grey Graham. (Adam and Charles Black, London, 1908)

[80] *An Act to Enable John Earl of Hopetoun, &c. To grant feus of certain Lands, Houses, &c. In the county of Dumfries, and to exchange and excamb the Lands therein mentioned*. (1760)

[81] *Tours in Scotland in 1745, 1743, 1760*. Richard Pococke, Bishop of Meath. (T. & A. Constable for the Scottish History Society, Edinburgh, 1887)

   Richard Pococke (1704 - 1765) was a traveller and Church of Ireland bishop of Ossory, of Elphin, and of Meath. His travels took him to Greece, Jerusalem, Egypt, Italy, France, and to every corner of the United Kingdom and Ireland.

[82] *An Extract of the Rev. Mr. John Wesley's Journal*. John Wesley (London, 1788)

   John Wesley (1703 - 1791) was an Anglican minister and Christian theologian who was an early leader in the Methodist movement. Wesley travelled constantly, generally on horseback, preaching two or three times a day. However by the time he visited Moffat he must surely have been travelling by coach.

[83] *The Beauties of Nature and Art Displayed in Tour through the World*. (J. Payne, London, 1863)

[84] *John Aiken M.D.* Mrs Herbert Martin. *Fraser's Magazine* May 1879

[85] *The Journals of James Boswell 1762-1795*. John Wain (Yale University Press, 1992)

[86] *A Tour in Scotland; MDCCLXIX*. Thomas Pennant (London, 1790)

   Thomas Pennant (1726 - 1798) was the greatest Welsh travel writer of his time and one of the best British topographical authors. Pennant had an overwhelming interest in natural history, and was regarded in his day as a leading zoologist.

John Walker (1731 – 1803), natural historian and Church of Scotland minister, was minister at Moffat from 1762 to 1783. In 1764 he was appointed to survey the Hebrides, and to make a report to the Society in Scotland for the Propagation of Christian Knowledge. John travelled 3,000 miles in seven months. His report, together with his 1771 tour and four other trips between 1766 and 1786, formed the basis of his manuscripts on the natural history of the Hebrides. In 1779, John was appointed regius professor of natural history and keeper of the university's museum at Edinburgh while retaining his clerical post at Moffat.

[87] *The Lyon in Mourning: a collection of speeches etc. by the Rev. Robert Forbes compiled by him 1746-1775.* Edited by Henry Paton (T. & A. Constable for the Scottish History Society, 1896)

Robert Forbes (1708 - 1775) was a Jacobite and the Scottish Episcopal Bishop of Ross and Caithness. He was arrested in 1745 on his way to join the Jacobite rising, and was imprisoned in the castles of Stirling and Edinburgh in 1746. In August 1769 he met secretly with Bishop Robert Gordon, head of the English nonjurors (those who refused to take an oath of allegiance to William and Mary or to their successors after the revolution of 1688), and 'Mr and Mrs Lyon' (Laurence and Margaret Oliphant of Gask) at Moffat, where they laid plans for a protestant marriage for Charles Edward in the hope of producing an acceptable Stuart heir.

[88] *The Life of John Buncle, Esq: Containing Various Observations ...Volume III.* Thomas Amory (London,1770)

[89] *Carruthers Thomson MSS.* Quoted in Annals of *the Three Dumfriesshire Dales.* W.A.J. Prevost. Lockerbie Press. (1954)

[90] *Traditions of Edinburgh.* Robert Chambers (W. & R. Chambers, Edinburgh, 1847)

Samuel Foote (1720 - 1777) was an actor and playwright with a gift for comic mimicry which made him a figure of both fear and delight on the London stage. He introduced the nonsense text "Grand Panjandrum" into the English language.

[91] *Present State of Husbandry in Scotland* (Volume II. Andrew Wight (Edinburgh, 1778)

[92] *Essays on the Trade, Commerce, Manufactures, and Fisheries of Scotland.* David Loch (W. & T. Ruddiman, Edinburgh,1778)

David Loch (d. 1780) was a merchant and ship owner from Leith. He became Inspector-General of Woollen Manufactures and Fisheries. His essays were commissioned by the Board of Manufactures and he was a strong proponent of "buy Scottish".

[93] *The Life of Mrs. Gooch.* Elizabeth Sarah Villa-Real Gooch. (London, 1792)

Elizabeth Gooch (1756 - about 1810) began life in a very wealthy family as Elizabeth Sarah Villa-Real but lost her fortune to a series of dissolute husbands. She ended up in the Fleet Prison for debtors before she published a series of novels. The "Real Life" was written in the form of an appeal for funds to pay off her debts.

[94] *The Christian Reformer; or, Unitarian Magazine and Review. New Series Volume XV.* (Edward Whitfield, London, 1859)

[95] *Memoir and Correspondence of the Late Sir James Edward Smith.* James Edward Smith (Longman, London, 1832)

Sir James Edward Smith (1759 - 1828) was an English botanist and founder of the Linnaean Society. During the early 1780s he enrolled in the medical course at the University of Edinburgh where he studied chemistry under Professor Joseph Black and natural history under Professor John Walker.

[96] *The Life of the Right Honourable Willielma, Viscountess Glenorchy.* Thomas Snell Jones. (William White and Co., Edinburgh, 1822)

[97] *Records of Female Piety.* James A. Huie (Oliver & Boyd, Edinburgh, 1841)

Lady Glenorchy (1741 - 1786) was the daughter of the Countess of Huntingdon. She had a conversion experience after a serious illness. Then after her husband's death she devoted her life to the spread of the evangelical cause, holding services for rich and poor and influencing many to enter the Church of Scotland ministry.

[98] *The Countess of Huntingdon and Her Circle.* Sarah Tytler. (Isaac Pitman, London, 1907)

Sarah Tytler was the pseudonym of Henrietta Keddie (1827 – 1914), who was a very prolific novelist and writer of children's stories.

[99] *James Currie – the Entire Stranger and Robert Burns.* Robert Donald (Oliver and Boyd, Edinburgh, 1963)

Dr. James Currie (1756 – 1805), physician and author, was born at Kirkpatrick Fleming. After an early and very adventurous life in Virginia, Currie qualified as a doctor and made a very successful career in Liverpool. On one of his visits to Scotland, he met Robert Burns and following Burns' death in 1796 he prepared the first full addition of Burns' work together with a biography.

[100] *A Tour in England and Scotland in 1785.* William Thomson. (G. & J. Robinson, London, 1788)

William Thomson wrote the account of his tour as "An English Gentleman". The 1791 edition of the book was published under the pseudonym of Thomas Newte Esq. of Devon.

[101] *A Tour Through the Highlands of Scotland, and the Hebride Isles, in 1786.* John Knox. (J. Walter, London, 1787)

[102] *Horæ subsecivæ.* John Brown. (Edmonston & Douglas, Edinburgh, 1862)

[103] *Gentleman's Magazine.* August 1787

[104] *Old Glasgow Essays.* John Oswald Mitchell (James Maclehose, Glasgow, 1905)

[105] *Voyage dans les trois royaumes d'Angleterre, d'Ecosse et d'Irlande, fait en 1788 et 1789.* Pierre Nicolas Chantreau (Paris, 1792)

> **Pierre Nicolas Chantreau** (1741 - 1808) was a historian, publicist, grammarian, and lexicographer. He was a firm believer in the principles of the French Revolution and at one time he worked in Spain as a secret agent.

[106] *Burns in Moffat.* John T. Johnstone (published in the Transactions of the Dumfries and Galloway Natural History and Antiquarian Society II.19, April 1907)

[107] *The Works of Robert Burns: Containing His Life.* Robert Burns, John Gibson Lockhart, James Currie (Judd, Loomis & Co., Hartford, 1837)

[108] *The Works of the Rev. John Wesley: Volume VI.* John Wesley (London, 1810)

[109] *Scotland delineated, or a geographical description of every shire in Scotland.* Robert Heron. (Edinburgh, 1791)

> **Robert Heron** (1764 - 1807) was a Scottish writer, born in New Galloway. While in Edinburgh he ended up in the debtors' prison before he published a series of books. In London he became a successful writer but then fell into bad habits. He spent the last years of his life imprisoned for debt in Newgate Prison.

[110] *Eastern Dumfriesshire: an archaeological landscape.* Royal Commission on the Ancient and Historical Monuments of Scotland (HMSO, 1997)

[111] *Ordnance Survey Six-Inch Map. Dumfriesshire 1861 Sheet xv.*

[112] *General View of the Agriculture, state of property, and improvements, in the county of Dumfries.* Dr. Singer (Edinburgh, 1812)

[113] **Sir George Clerk-Maxwell** (1715-1784) was born in Edinburgh, the son of Sir John Clerk of Penicuick. Sir George owned Dumcrieff from 1737 to 1782. He was distinguished by his spirited attempts to further the commercial interests of Scotland with interests in agriculture, fisheries, and manufacturing. In 1763 he became commissioner of the customs in Scotland. On marrying his cousin he assumed his wife's name of Maxwell as well as his own.

[114] *Memoir of the Life, Writings, and Correspondence of James Currie M.D., F.R.S. of Liverpool.* William Wallace Currie (Longman, London, 1831)

[115] *The Poetical Works of Janet Little, the Scotch Milkmaid* (John and Peter Wilson, Ayr, 1792)

[116] *Letters on a Tour through Various Parts of Scotland in the Year 1792.* John Lettice (London, 1794)

The Rev. John Lettice (1737 - 1832) was a Cambridge don.

[117] *Memorials of Moffat Parish.* Gilchrist and Shannon (June 1971)

[118] *The Waverley Novels: With the Author's Last Corrections and Addition. Volume V.* John Gibson Lockhart. (Carey and Hart, Philadelphia, 1847)

James Skene (1775 - 1864), born in Aberdeen, was a talented amateur artist and antiquary. He became acquainted with Walter Scott when they were both young advocates in Parliament House, Edinburgh.

[119] *Observations on the Different Breeds of Sheep and the State of Sheep Farming in the Southern Districts of Scotland.* John Naysmyth (for the Society for Improvement of British Wool). (Edinburgh, 1795)

[120] *Catalogue of the Papers of James Boswell at Yale University.* Marion S. Pottle. (Edinburgh University Press)

[121] *Dumfries Weekly Journal.* 4th November 1794

[122] The location of Rae's Inn was researched in some detail by John T. Johnstone and he concluded that it was somewhere close to the present site of the Buccleuch Arms. *Transactions of the Dumfries and Galloway Natural History and Antiquities Society 18th April 1907*

[123] *Diary of a Tour Through Great Britain in 1795.* Rev. William MacRitchie (London, 1897)

William MacRitchie was a Presbyterian minister who, in 1795, travelled from Perthshire to London and back.

[124] *Life of Robert Owen - Volume 1.* Robert Owen. (Effingham Wilson, London, 1857)

Robert Owen (1771 - 1858) was a Welsh social reformer and one of the founders of socialism and the cooperative movement. His experiment at New Lanark led to it becoming a much frequented place of pilgrimage for social reformers.

[125] *The Tour of the Duke of Somerset, and the Rev. J. H. Michell, through parts of England, Wales, and Scotland, in the year 1795.* Rev. John Henry Michell. (R. Clay, London, 1845)

[126] *Amazing Grace: the Great Days of Dukes.* E. S. Turner. (Michael Joseph, London, 1975) [The phrase "ducal irresponsibility" is Turner's and may reflect his poorly-disguised dislike of dukedom.]

[127] *Journal of a Tour through Scotland in 1798* by John Housman, published in *The Monthly Magazine* (London, 1800)

[128] *A Companion and Useful Guide to the Beauties of Scotland...* Hon. Mrs Murray (London, 1799)

The Honourable Mrs. Sarah Murray of Kensington was a topographical writer.

[129] *Pigot's Directory of Dumfries-shire 1837.* Facsimile Reprint (G.C. Publishers, Wigtown, 1996)

[130] *Observations on a Tour Through the Highlands and Part of the Western Isles.* Thomas Garnett (John Stockdale, London, 1800)

Thomas Garnett, MD (1766 - 1802) was Professor of Chemistry and Natural Philosophy at Anderson's College, Glasgow (now part of Strathclyde University) between 1796 and 1799. In 1799 he left to become the first professor of the London Royal Institution.

[131] *The Edinburgh Literary Journal or Weekly register of Criticism and Belles Lettres.* A contribution by James Hogg (1829).

[132] *Dumfries Weekly Journal* 6th December 1803.

[133] *Horæ subsecivæ.* John Brown (Edmonston & Douglas, Edinburgh, 1862)

John Brown (1784 - 1858) was a Scottish divine. In 1835 he was appointed one of the professors in the theological hall of the Secession church.

[134] *Edinburgh Magazine: Or Literary Miscellany* 21st October 1802

[135] *A Family Tour Through the British Empire: Containing Some Accounts of Its ...* Priscilla Wakefield (Darton, Harvey & Darton, London, 1804)

Priscilla Wakefield (1751 -1 832), author and philanthropist, was the aunt of the prison reformer Elizabeth Fry. She wrote educational books, particularly for a younger readership, and she also wrote about the problems inherent in contemporary female education.

[136] *A Collection of Modern and Contemporary Voyages and Travels. Volume II.* (Richard Phillips,London,1805)

[137] *An excursion to the Highlands of Scotland and the English Lakes, with recollections, descriptions, and references to historical facts.* Joseph Mawman. (London, 1805)

[138] *The Beauties of Scotland: Containing a Clear and Full Account of the ...* Robert Forsyth (Edinburgh, 1805)

[139] *Folklore and Genealogies of Uppermost Nithsdale.* William Wilson. (Dumfries, Courier and Herald Press, 1904)

[140] *Reproduced from Observations on a Tour Through the Highlands and Part of the Western Isles.* Thomas Garnett (John Stockdale, London, 1800)

[141] *Moffat: Early Roads and Coaching Days.* Thomas Henderson. (Annandale Observer Press, Annan, 1960)

[142] *Edinburgh Annual Register.* January 1808.

[143] *Thomas Carlyle Reminiscences.* Thomas Carlyle (MacMillan, London, 1887)

[144] *Journal of a Tour and Residence in Great Britain, During the Years 1810 and 1811.* Louis Simond. (Constable, Edinburgh, 1815)
Louis Simond (1767 - 1831). This book was originally written in English; prepared for publication in French, but not issued in French until 1816, under the title: *Voyage d'un français en Angleterre.*

[145] *Blackwood's Edinburgh Magazine October 1817* (William Blackwood, Edinburgh, 1817)

John Finlay (1782 – 1810), poet, was born to poor parents at Glasgow. He was educated in one of the Glasgow academies, and at the age of fourteen entered the university where he studied Latin, Greek, and philosophy. He had as a classmate John Wilson ('Christopher North'), who states that he "distinguished himself above most of his contemporaries". While only nineteen and still at the university Finlay published *Wallace, or The Vale of Ellerslie, and other Poems* (1802),

[146] *A Grammar of the Principles and Practice of Chemistry.* Richard Phillips. (London, 1810)

[147] *Think's-I-to-Myself, a Serio-ludicro,Tragico-comico Tale.* Thinks I to Myself Who? (Sherwood, Neely and Jones, London, 1811)

[148] *Letters from Scotland: by an English commercial traveller* (Longman, London, 1817)

[149] *Carlyle Till Marriage 1795 to 1826.* David Alec Wilson (Kessinger Publishing, Whitefish, Montana, 2004)

[150] *Travels Through England, Wales, & Scotland, in the Year 1816.* Samuel Heinrich Spiker. (London, 1820)

[151] *Annals of the Three Dumfriesshire Dales.* W.A.J. Prevost. (Lockerbie Press, 1954)

[152] *Moffat 17th to 20th Century.* Jane L. Boyd (Moffat Museum, 1987)

[153] *A Continuation of the Memoirs of Charles Mathews, Comedian.* Mrs. Matthews. (Lea & Blanchard, Philadelphia, 1839)

Charles Matthews (1776 - 1835) was a celebrated Victorian comic actor whose work was much admired by young Charles Dickens. He regularly appeared in the major London theatres.

[154] *A Topographical Dictionary of Scotland.* David Webster (Edinburgh, 1819)

[155] Reproduced from *Annals of Three Dumfriesshire Dales.* W.A.J.Prevost (Lockerbie Press, Lockerbie, 1954)

[156] *Memoir and Correspondence of Mrs. Grant of Laggan.* Anne MacVicar Grant (Longman, Edinburgh, 1845)

Anne Macvicar Grant (1755 - 1838), letter-writer, essayist, and poet, spent the first eighteen years her life near Albany, New York. She settled in Scotland in 1773, married in 1779, had 12 children by 1799, was widowed in 1801, and went on to pursue a highly successful literary career.

[157] *The Wordsworth-Laing Letters, Modern Language Review* Vol. 46. No 1.

[158] *The Kaleidoscope or Literary and Scientific Mirror.* 18th March 1823

[159] *Glasgow Medical Journal. Volume 1.* (David Allan & Co., Glasgow, 1828)

[160] *Some Unpublished Letters of Sir Walter Scott.* Walter Scott, Davidson Cook (Blackwell, London, 1932)

[161] *The Derby Mercury* 21st September 1825

[162] *The Times* 8th October 1825

Charles Green (1785 - 1870) was the United Kingdom's most famous balloonist of the 19th Century. He experimented with coal gas as a cheaper and more readily available alternative to hydrogen for lifting power. His first ascent, in 1821, was in a coal gas balloon. He became a professional balloonist and had made 200 ascents by 1835. In 1836, he set a major long distance record in the balloon "Royal Vauxhall", flying overnight from Vauxhall Gardens in London to Weilburgin Germany, a distance of 480 miles: this record was not broken until 1907.

[163] This entry in Sir Walter Scott's diary was published in *Memoirs of the Life of Sir Walter Scott, Bart* by John Gibson Lockhart (Ticknor & Fields, Boston, 1837)

[164] *The Journal of Sir Walter Scott from the Original Manuscript at Abbotsford.* (Burt Franklin, New York, 1890)

[165] *A Medical Sketch of Dumfriesshire.* J. Erskine Gibson. (John Sinclair, Dumfries, 1827)

[166] This recollection is by John McDiarmid and is included in his *A Guide to Moffat* (McDiarmid, Dumfries, 1852)

William Ritchie (1781 – 1831), was born at Lundin Links, Fife. He was a solicitor who co-founded *The Scotsman* with Charles McLaren in 1817. From 1817 to 1831 Ritchie was the first editor of the newspaper. John McDiarmid was a close friend of Ritchie.

[167] *The Picture of Scotland Volume 1.* Robert Chambers. (William Tait, Edinburgh, 1827)

Robert Chambers (1802 – 1871), born in Peebles, was an author, geologist, and publisher. He joined with his brother William as partners in the publishing firm of W. & R. Chambers.

[168] *The Caledonian Mercury* 5th July 1827

[169] *A Speech in Moffat on the Beauties of Moffat and the Usefulness of That Excellent Mineral Well*. Henry MacMinn. The speech was published in 1831 with the text of other speeches , as *Speeches on various Public Occasions during the last Thirty Years*, and dedicated to King William IV. Reproduced in part in *The Moffat Times, Register and Annandale Observer* 9th May 1874.

> **Henry Macminn** of Lochfield, had a prolific fund of eloquence, that enabled him to dilate easily and effectively on all manner of subjects. Never was the local Demosthenes more fervid and exalted than when toasting the memory of Burns. At a festive meeting held in 1822, on the anniversary of the poet's natal day, Mr. Macminn declared that no sooner had the bard reached the summit of Mount Parnassus, "than he was surrounded by the gods, who with one voice pronounced that Burns should take the right hand of Jove himself, in the first chariot of fame, as a poet of the age."

[170] *Trial of William Burke and Helen McDougal: Before the High Court of Justiciary*. (Robert Buchanan, Edinburgh, 1829)

[171] *West Port Murders: or, An Authentic Account of the Atrocious Murders*. (Thomas Ireland, Edinburgh, 1829)

[172] *History of the Burgh of Dumfries*. William McDowall (T.C. Farries, Dumfries, 1986)

[173] *Leigh's New Pocket Road-book of Scotland*. Samuel Leigh. (Samuel Leigh, London, 1829)

[174] *The Scotsman* 20th May 1829

[175] *The Manual for Invalids*, by A Physician (Edward Bull, London, 1829)

[176] *Dumfries Times* 16th April 1834

[177] *Chambers Edinburgh Journal*. September 1832

[178] *Dumfries Times* 28th November 1838

[179] *The Mirror of Literature, Amusement, and Instruction*. Volume 19, No. 536, 1832.

[180] *Essay on curling, and artificial pond making*. J. Cairnie (W.R. McPhun, Glasgow, 1833)

> **John Cairnie** (1769 - ?) had returned to Scotland after service in India in the course of which he had lost an arm. He settled at Curling Hall, Largs with the intention of spending his summers sailing and his winters curling. His ideas for the standardisation of the game found favour amongst Scottish curlers and in 1838 he was elected as the first President of the Royal Caledonian Curling Club.

[181] *The Carlyle Letters Online*. Letter from Jane Welsh Carlyle to Helen Welsh dated 1st April 1836 (www.carlyleletters.dukejournals.org/)

[182] *The New Statistical Account of Scotland* (William Blackwood and Sons, Edinburgh, 1845.)

[183] *The Times* 4th December 1835

[184] *The Scottish tourist, and Itinerary.* "Scottish Tourist". (Stirling, Kenney & Co., Edinburgh, 1836)

[185] *The Quarterly Journal of Agriculture. Volume VII June 1836-March 1837.* (William Blackwood, Edinburgh, 1837)

[186] *The Scotsman* 25th June 1836

[187] *Tourist's Guide Through Scotland: Upon a New and Improved Plan.* John Anderson. (Edinburgh, 1837)

[188] *A Bibliographical, Antiquarian and Picturesque Tour in the Northern Counties.* Thomas Frognall Dibdin. (London, 1838)

Thomas Frognall Dibdin (1776 - 1847), was an English bibliographer and clergyman.

[189] *Homes and Haunts of the Most Eminent British Poets.* William Howitt. (Routledge, Warne & Routledge, London, 1847)

William Howitt (1792 – 1879) was an English author. His works were marked by his acute habits of observation and his genuine love of nature.

[190] *The Scotsman* 4th July 1838

[191] *Dumfries and Galloway Standard* 20th May 1846

[192] *Nelsons' Hand-book to Scotland: for tourists.* John Marius Wilson. (Nelson, London, 1860)

[193] *Lizars' Scottish Tourist: A Guide to the Picturesque Scenery, Antiquities etc.* William Home Lizars. (W.H. Lizars, Edinburgh, 1850)

[194] *The Carlyle Letters Online.* Letter from Thomas Carlyle to John Greig dated 17th April 1847 (www.carlyleletters.dukejournals.org/)

Thomas Carlyle (1795 – 1881), born in Ecclefechan, was an essayist, satirist, and historian, whose work was hugely influential during the Victorian era.

John Aitken Carlyle (1801-1879), a doctor who spent much time travelling with wealthy patients, was Thomas Carlyle's brother. He married Phoebe Watts at Moffat in 1852 and the newly-weds took up residence at Moffat House.

[195] *The Scotsman* 18th October 1845

[196] *The Scotsman* 21st June 1845

[197] *Tait's Edinburgh Magazine Volume XIV*. William Tait and Christian Isobel Johnstone (Edinburgh, 1847)

[198] *Letters from the Wells, Visit to Moffat, Its Spas and Neighbourhood*. William Wallace Fyfe. (J.D. Lowe, Edinburgh, 1848)

[199] *The Spas of England, and Principal Sea-bathing Places*. Augustus Bozzi Granville. (Henry Colburn, London, 1841) and *The Spas of Germany*. Augustus Bozzi Granville (Henry Colburn, London, 1838)

[200] Originally published in the *North British Mail* and later reproduced in the *Manchester Times and Gazette* 18th July 1848.

[201] *Tait's Edinburgh Magazine for 1849*. William Tait (Edinburgh, 1849)

[202] *The Times* May 17th 1849

[203] *Hogg's Weekly Instructor*. James Hogg. (James Hogg, Edinburgh, 1848)

James Hogg (1806 – 1888), son of the poet, was a Scottish publisher. In Edinburgh in 1849 he made the acquaintance of Thomas de Quincey who contributed his *Autobiographic Sketches* to Hogg's publications, and then agreed with Hogg to bring out his Collected Works. Hogg later moved to London where, with his sons, he pursued a successful publishing business.

[204] *Fairfoul's Guide to Moffat*. Thomas M. Fairfoul. (Thomas Fairfoul, Moffat, 1879)

[205] *Autumnal Rambles Among the Scottish Mountains*. Rev. Thomas Grierson (James Hogg, Edinburgh, 1851)

Rev. Thomas Grierson was the minister of Kirkbean Church. In his spare time he was a fanatical hill walker covering vast distances by foot from one end of the country to another.

[206] *Dumfries and Galloway Standard* 30th October 1850

[207] *Angler's Guide to the Rivers & Lochs of Scotland*. Robert Blakey (Thomas Murray, Glasgow, 1854)

Dr. Robert Blakey (1795 - 1878) was born at Morpeth, the son of a mechanic in a cotton factory. In politics, Robert became a Cobbettite Radical and he was a personal friend of William Cobbett, the political reformer. He was involved for many years in the agitation that led to the Reform Act of 1832. In 1848 Robert was appointed to the post of professor of Logic and Metaphysics at Queen's College, Belfast, but illness led to his dismissal from that post in 1851 by which time he was living in Academy Road, Moffat while he had another residence in Glasgow. During this time he wrote two new books, "*The Angler's Complete Guide to the Rivers and Lakes of England*" (1853), "*Angler's Guide to the Rivers and Lochs of Scotland*" (1854) and "*The History of Political Literature*" (1855).

[208] Reproduced in the *Dumfries and Galloway Standard* 1st September 1852

William Keddie (1809 - 1877) was born in Peebles. At the age of 23 he became sub-editor of the *Glasgow Scottish Guardian* and in a few years he was the editor. His abiding interest was natural history and when the *Scottish Guardian* went out of business he lectured on that subject, eventually becoming Professor of Natural History at Glasgow University.

[209] *A Selection from the Letters of Lydia Ann Barclay, a Minister of the Gospel.* Lydia Ann Barclay (George Harrison, Manchester, 1862)

[210] *A Guide to Moffat Embracing the Surrounding Scenery etc.* John McDiarmid. (J. McDiarmid & Son, Dumfries, 1852)

John McDiarmid (1790 – 1852), newspaper editor, was born in Glasgow. In January 1817 he was one of those who prepared the first issue of *The Scotsman* and in the same month he moved to Dumfries to become editor of the *Dumfries and Galloway Courier*, which he edited until his death. During his life he formed friendships with Sir Walter Scott, James Hogg and John Wilson.

[211] *The Carlyle Letters Online.* Letter from Jane Welsh Carlyle to Thomas Carlyle dated 8th July 1853. (www.carlyleletters.dukejournals.org/)

Jane Welsh Carlyle (1801 - 1866) was Thomas Carlyle's wife. The daughter of a doctor from Haddington and Grace Welsh from Caplegill, she revealed herself in her letters as a formidable intellectual talent. She suffered from severe depression, particularly in her later years.

[212] *The Moffat Register and Annandale Observer* 11th July 1857

[213] *The Carlyle Letters Online.* Letter from Thomas Carlyle to John Carlyle dated 13th October 1854 (www.carlyleletters.dukejournals.org/)

[214] *Moffat: Its Walks and Wells.* William Keddie. (Blackie, Glasgow, 1854)

[215] *Dumfries and Galloway Standard* 18th October 1854

[216] *Stewart's Practical Angler*, published in *Blackwood's Edinburgh Magazine Volume 81*, June 1857

[217] *Memoir of Norman MacLeod,D.D.* Rev. Donald MacLeod (R. Worthington, New York, 1874)

[218] *Dumfries and Galloway Standard 22nd June 1872.*

Dr. Norman Macleod (1812 - 1872) was a Scottish divine who became a minister in Glasgow in 1851 where he made great efforts to ameliorate the conditions of working people. He was known as one of the most eloquent preachers in Scotland and in 1857 he was appointed chaplain to Queen Victoria with whom he became a great favourite. In 1867 he was Moderator of the General Assembly. His many works included *"The Earnest Student"* (a biography of John Mackintosh) and *"The Gold Thread"*, published in 1861.

[219] Reproduced in part in the *Moffat Register and Annandale Observer* September 1857

[220] *Fairfoul's Guide to Moffat.* Thomas M. Fairfoul. (Thomas Fairfoul, Moffat, 1879) **Thomas Fairfoul**, bookseller and stationer, ran his business from a shop in Moffat High Street. He was also the librarian for the Moffat Subscription Library which, by 1879, contained about 4,000 titles.

[221] *Moffat Register and Annandale Observer* 14th August 1858

[222] *Old Faces in New Masks.* Robert Blakey and George Cruikshank (W .Kent, London, 1859)

[223] *Whitehaven Herald* 21st August 1858

[224] *The Dumfries Courier* 17th May 1859

[225] *The Dumfries Herald* 20th May 1859

[226] *Dunfermline Journal* 30th September 1859

[227] This unattributed quotation is provided in *Moffat ..... A Backward Glance.* Sheila Forman. (Lochar Publishing, Moffat, 1949)

[228] *The Scotsman* 3rd November 1859

[229] *New Sporting Magazine*, June 1861 and September 1861

[230] *The Ferns of Moffat; a collection of the ferns found in the neighbourhood of Moffat, with popular descriptions and localities of all the known species.* J.C. Moffatt. (Moffat, 1863)

[231] *The Moffat Fern-Album.* William Carruthers. (Moffat, 1863)

[232] *The Moffat Register and Annandale Observer* 6th October 1860

[233] *The Scotsman* 30th March 1860

[234] *Meditations on Dyspepsia*, published in *Blackwood's Edinburgh Magazine Vol. 90*, October 1861

[235] *Glasgow Herald* 4th November 1861

[236] *The Scotsman* 24th August 1864

[237] *The Scotsman* 27th June 1859

[238] *The Scotsman* 10th August 1863

[239] *The Caledonian Mercury* 8th July 1864

[240] *The Scotsman* 13th June 1864

[241] *Glasgow Herald* 17th September 1864

242 *Scotland Described.* Alexander Murray. (Alexander Murray, Glasgow, 1866)

243 *The Scotsman* 15th May 1863

244 *The Harvest of the Sea.* James Glass Bertram. (John Murray, London, 1865)

245 *The New Sporting Magazine* (September 1866)

246 *The Scotsman* 1865

247 *Moffat Times* 4th September 1869

248 *Moffat Times* 4th September 1869

249 *The Scotsman* 21st June 1869

250 *Moffat Times* 30th October 1869

251 *Moffat Times* 13th November 1869

252 *Dumfries and Galloway Standard* 5th October 1870

253 *The Strange Adventures of a Phaeton.* William Black. *MacMillan's Magazine 27.* April 1873.

    William Black (1841 – 1898) was a novelist born in Glasgow. In his own lifetime Black's novels were immensely popular and widely read, and were compared favourably with those of Anthony Trollope.

254 *Moffat Times* 13th July 1872

255 *Moffat Times* 27th July 1872

256 *Moffat Times* 28th September 1872

257 *Lord Lister.* Sir John Godlee Rickman. (Clarendon Press, Oxford, 1924)

    Joseph Jackson Lister, 1st Baron Lister, (1827 - 1812) was born at Upton in Essex. Aged 25, he graduated with honours as Bachelor of Medicine and entered the Royal College of Surgeons. In 1854, Joseph began working with the surgeon James Syme at the University of Edinburgh. He married Agnes, Syme's daughter. As a result of his research, Lister published a series of articles in *The Lancet* on the *Antiseptic Principle in the Practice of Surgery*, describing the benefits of using carbolic acid for the sterilisation of surgical instruments and the need for surgeons to wash their hands and to wear gloves.

258 *The Scotsman* 15th May 1875

259 *The Free Library: Its History and Present Condition.* John Ogle. (George Allan, London, 1897)

Stephen Mitchell (1789 - 1874) was born in Linlithgow into a long-established family of tobacco merchants and burghers. On the death of his father in 1820 he took over the running of the business, which transferred to Glasgow in 1825. Even after becoming part of the Imperial Tobacco Group in 1901 Mitchell's continued to trade under the name of Stephen Mitchell and Son until it was eventually absorbed by WD & HO Wills in 1957.

[260] *Moffat Times* 19th September1874

[261] *The Scotsman* 20th October 1875

[262] The *Chemical News and Journal of Physical Science*. 8th January 1875

[263] *The Scotsman* 16th October 1876

[264] *The Scotsman* 13th March 1878

[265] *Chambers' Journal of Popular Literature, Science and Arts* . September 1878.

[266] *The Scotsman* 17th May 1881

[267] *Anglers' Evenings – Papers by Members of the Manchester Anglers Association.* Second Series. (Abel Heywood, Manchester, 1882)

[268] *Nautilus in Scotland: A Tricycle Tour of 2,462 Miles.* "Nautilus". (Simpkin, Marshall & Co, London, 1882)

[269] *A Drive Through England or a Thousand Miles of Road Travel.* James John Hissey. (Richard Bentley, London, 1885)

[270] *The Scotsman* 29th December 1886

[271] *Moffat News and Annandale Herald.* 18th December 1896

William Allan (1837 - 1903) was born in Dundee. He was M.P. for Gateshead-on-Tyne from 1893 to 1903 and he was knighted in 1902. In Parliament he was a supporter of navy reforms and he frequently asked technical questions about steam boilers which gave him the nickname of "Boiler Bill". Perhaps as a visual pun, William wore a Buffalo Bill hat in the House of Commons. He was also a poet with many of verses, including some about the Moffat area, being privately published.

[272] *The Scotsman* 4th April 1896

[273] *Dumfries and Galloway Standard* 22nd September 1897

[274] Glasgow *Evening News*, published in the *Moffat News and Annandale Herald* 4th June 1897.

[275] *The Scotsman* 30th September 1899

[276] *Birkhill: Reminiscence by a Liverpool Merchant.* Charles Robert Bryden McGilchrist. (James Lewis, Selkirk, 1899)

[277] *Moffat News and Annandale Herald.* 5th January 1900

[278] *Prospectus of the Moffat Hydropathic and Pension with Guide to the District* (1897)

Additional Sources

Moffat Place-Names

The Place Names of Dumfriesshire. Sir Edward Johnson-Ferguson (Dumfries, 1935)

Scottish Place-Names: Their Study and Significance. W.F.H. Nicolaisen (London, 1976)

Annals of Three Dumfriesshire Dales. W.A.J. Prevost (Herald Press, Lockerbie, 1954)

Artefacts and Coins left by Roman Visitors

An Inventory of Roman and Roman provincial origin in the *Proceedings of the Society of Antiquaries of Scotland 116..* James Curle. (1932)

Eastern Dumfriesshire: an archaeological landscape. Royal Commission on the Ancient and Historical Monuments of Scotland (HMSO, 1997)

Roman Coins Found in Scotland in the *Proceedings of the Society of Antiquaries of Scotland.* Anne S. Robertson.

Roman and medieval coins found in Scotland, 1988-95 in the *Proceedings of the Society of Antiquaries of Scotland 127 (1997).* J. D. Bateson & N. M. M^{c}Q. Holmes

Drove Roads

The Drove Roads of Scotland. A.R.B. Haldane (Thomas Nelson and Sons, Edinburgh, 1952)

The Drove Road into Annandale in *Transactions of the Dumfries and Galloway Natural History and Antiquarian Society 3rd. Series XXXI 1952-53.*W.A.J. Prevost.

Inns and Hotels

The Buildings of Scotland: Dumfries and Galloway. John Gifford (Penguin, London, 1996)

Moffat: Early Roads and Coaching Days. Thomas Henderson (Annandale Observer Press, Lockerbie, 1960)

Burns in Moffat. John T. Johnstone (published in the Transactions of the Dumfries and Galloway Natural History and Antiquarian Society II.19, April 1907)

Dumfries and Galloway Standard 2nd January 1878 and 9th March 1881

Goats

Jane Boyd's Old Moffat. Jane Boyd (Upland Vision, Moffat, 1998)

Carrifran Wildwood Project: Native woodland restoration in the Southern Uplands of Scotland - Management Plan. Wildwood Group of the Borders Forest Trust. (Borders Forest Trust, Jedburgh, October 2000)

Old Statistical Account of Scotland (1791-99): Parish of Moffat

New Statistical Account of Scotland (1834-45): Parish of Moffat

The Devil Drink

Scottish Pubs – Heather Ale (www.scottishpubs.co.uk)

General View of the Agriculture of the County of Dumfries: With Observations on the Means of its Improvement. Bryce Johnston (Board of Agriculture and Internal Improvement, London, 1894)

Annals of Three Dumfriesshire Dales. W.A.J. Prevost (Herald Press, Lockerbie, 1954)

The Music of Moffat

The Siller Gun: A Poem, in Five Cantos. John Mayne (William Blackwood, Edinburgh, 1836)

The Moffat Register and Annandale Observer. Various issues between 1857 and 1870.

Markets, Fairs, Sales and Shows

Moffat Past and Present. John Brown (J. Menzies, Edinburgh 1873)

History of Moffat with frequent notices of Moffatdale and Annandale. W. Robertson Turnbull (W. P. Nimmo, Edinburgh, 1871)

Upper Annandale in the 17th Century. John T. Johnstone

The Scotsman and *Moffat Register and Annandale Observer:* various editions between 1840 and 1880.

Beld Craig Linn and Garpol Glen

Moffat Times 24th July 1869 (Garpol Glen)

Moffat Times 17th July 1869 (Beld Craig Linn)

Moffat Past and Present. John Brown (J. Menzies, Edinburgh 1873)

Observations on a Tour Through the Highlands and Part of the Western Isles. Thomas Garnett (John Stockdale, London, 1800)

The Moffat Railway

Dumfries and Galloway Standard 4th April 1883

Encyclopaedia of British Railway Companies. Christopher Christopher, London. 1990

Visitor Numbers and House Building

The Moffat Times and *Moffat Register and Annandale Observer:* various editions between 1857 and 1880.

Moffat Past and Present. John Brown (J. Menzies, Edinburgh 1873)

Disease and Life Expectancy

Scotland's People (www.scotlandspeople.gov.uk)

History of the Burgh of Dumfries. William McDowall (T.C. Farries, Dumfries, 1986)

Eminent Engineers

The Life of Joseph Locke, Civil Engineer, M.P., F.R.S. Joseph Devey. (Richard Bentley, London, 1862)

The North British Railway. Cuthbert Hamilton Ellis (Ian Allan, London, 1955)

Scotland Bitter-Sweet. James Drawbell (Macdonald and Co., London, 1972)

Moffat Town Criers

Moffat Times, Register and Upper Annandale Advertiser 7th May 1870

Moffat Times 2nd March 1872

Charles Lapworth and the Moffat Series

The Moffat Series. Charles Lapworth. Published in the *Quarterly Journal of the Geological Society of London. 34 (*1878)

The Lapworth Museum (www.lapworth.bham.ac.uk/)

Posts, Telegraphs and Telephones

Dumfries and Galloway Standard 5th February 1870

Moffat Times 11th December 1869

The Telephone Museum (www.telephonesuk.co.uk/ttm_mk.htm)

BT Archives, Holborn Telephone Exchange, London WC1V 7EE